THE COMPLETE G

George Mic

MW01143382

Copyright © 1998 Omnibus Press
(A Division of Book Sales Limited)

Edited by Robert Dimery
Book designed by Hilite Design & Reprographics Limited
Picture research by Nikki Russell

ISBN: 0.7119.6822.5
Order No: OP48060

Exclusive Distributors:
Book Sales Limited, 8/9 Frith Street, London W1V 5TZ, UK.
Music Sales Corporation, 257 Park Avenue South, New York, NY 10010, USA.
Music Sales Pty Limited, 120 Rothschild Avenue, Rosebery, NSW 2018, Australia.

To the Music Trade only:
Music Sales Limited, 8/9, Frith Street, London W1V 5TZ, UK.

Photo credits: Front cover: Retna. All other pictures supplied by LFI and Rex Features.

Every effort has been made to trace the copyright holders of the photographs in this book but one or two were unreachable. We would be grateful if the photographers concerned would contact us.

Printed in Great Britain by Printwise (Haverhill) Limited, Suffolk

A catalogue record for this book is available from the British Library.

Visit Omnibus Press at http://www.omnibuspress.com

OMNIBUS PRESS
LONDON · NEW YORK · SYDNEY

CONTENTS

INTRODUCTION

'I keep fame in a little box and sometimes I take it out and enjoy it.' George Michael has always lived life at opposite ends of the celebrity spectrum, alternating between being an outstanding natural performer and a media-shy recluse. He has won countless awards including Grammys and BRITS, become the youngest ever recipient of the Ivor Novello Songwriting Award and been the first male artist to sell a million on CD format. Numerous charities have benefited from his generous contributions, especially causes related to AIDS awareness, the homeless and famine relief. Despite the above accolades, George's recent personal complications, bereavements and indiscretions have led him to believe that his carefree time with the teen pop sensation Wham! was the happiest period of his life; 'we were two kids at the top of a dream'.

Shirlie Kemp (née Holliman), former dolly-bird dancer with Wham! once stated, 'George Michael is someone who has been made up.' Indeed George made his début on the 25th June, 1963 as Georgios Kyriacos Panayiotou. His close-knit, half Greek-Cypriot family provided a stable, yet upwardly mobile environment which enabled him to flourish as a studious, self-absorbed and content little boy. The turning point came when he encountered his alter-ego, Andrew Ridgeley, in his first year at Bushey Meads Comprehensive School. Ridgeley was super-confident, handsome and determined to be famous, be it as a swanky pop star or a heroic footballer, and much to the young George's parents' dismay the pair soon became inseparable. The intense bond was strengthened by a shared sense of humour and a joint love of their recently purchased copies of the LP *Goodbye Yellow Brick Road* by Elton John.

In a bid for teenage stardom, the duo joined forces with Andrew's younger brother Paul and school friends David Mortimer and Andrew Leaver to form ska-influenced group, The Executive. Although short-lived, band life gave the boys a taste for fame and following the group's inevitable demise in 1980, the musical partnership of George and Andrew metamorphosed into Wham! Andrew later divulged in *Wham! The Official Biography* by Luke Crampton: 'Getting George into a band at 16 was one of my most important contributions.'

Ignoring constant pressure from his father to 'get a proper job', George defiantly installed a rented portastudio in Andrew's front room and Wham! set about recording their first demo tape for the princely sum of £20. The badly produced result eventually landed on the doormat of Mark Dean, a Ridgeley family friend and record industry whiz-kid. Sensing a spark of genius within the twenty second snippets of hits-in-the-making 'Careless Whisper' and 'Wham! Rap', Dean snatched up the teenage group as a figurehead for his fledgling Innervision label, a subsidiary of CBS. The resulting contract was a tough deal all round but a big break for three young men who at that stage were none too concerned with any legal implications and all too fixated with the prospect of appearing on *Top Of The Pops*.

'Wham! Rap' was the first release, and although the initial chart placings were disappointing, the single was well received by the press with *NME* encouragingly describing it as a 'spirited fist shaken in the face of adult apathy'. A second single, 'Young Guns' swiftly followed and rocketed to Number 2, establishing Wham! as the latest and greatest in a succession of fun-loving Eighties pop bands. Their success was consolidated with a tour featuring 'knobbly kneed MC' Capital Radio DJ, Gary Crowley as the warm-up act, and displaying the tantalising talents of female backing dancers, Pepsi De Marque and Shirlie Holliman.

The rest is pop history. George Michael swiftly took full control with the learned aid of his trusted publishers Bryan Morrison and Dick Leahy, and perspicacious managers Simon Napier-Bell and Jazz

Summers. Upon the disintegration of their contract with Innervision, Wham! signed to another CBS subsidary, Epic, and went on to top the charts and tour world-wide, notably becoming the first Western pop group to perform in China.

The first indication that George Michael might go on to achieve greater things came with the release of his first solo single, the heart-stopping 'Careless Whisper', during Wham!'s second album, *Make It Big*. Early on the boys had decided that Andrew Ridgeley would take a back seat in the writing, recording and producing aspect, instead overseeing the band's visual style and image. George's songwriting skills were rapidly improving into the work of a true craftsman, and his impressive vocal dynamism was honoured with the invitation to perform for Band Aid, and later at Live Aid. In a year when Wham! were popularly considered to be a laughing stock by more 'serious'-minded musicians, Live Aid made a genuine star of George, providing him with the credibility he so desperately sought, and proving that now was the time to break free from the constraints of his group.

The Wham! split was mutually agreed by George and Andrew in November 1985. They endeavoured to go out with a bang, organising a spectacular, one-off farewell concert entitled 'The Final'. Andrew went on to pursue a rocky course in motor racing, releasing just one equally unstable solo album, *Son Of Albert*, in 1990. At the time of the split George was confident that he could forge an auspicious solo career, cuttingly responding to *Number 1* magazine's query about Ridgeley's departure; 'Well, it's not going to damage my musical output, Andrew knew he was there for a purpose.'

Following a period of excess bingeing and depression, George pulled himself together and released his début solo album, aptly titled *Faith*. Proving that scandal sells records, George's first single 'I Want Your Sex' provoked controversy and criticism but simultaneously boosted his persona in the public eye. Having sold himself so brazenly for the *Faith* album and ensuing tour,

George about-turned and retreated from the intrusive side of celebrity life. His next venture was a more mature and profound album, *Listen Without Prejudice Volume I*, which was an attempt to shake his frivolous pop star image of the past. Poor sales of the album incited George to challenge his record company, Sony (who had recently bought out CBS), for 'unreasonable restraint of trade'. The opposing sides were consequently tied to a lengthy stretch of bitter legal wranglings before the companies Virgin and DreamWorks collectively paid $40 million to release George from his contract. The negative publicity surrounding the case has been attributed to inspire the recently released film, *Bring Me The Head Of Mavis Davis*.

George returned to the music scene in 1996 with the release of *Older*, which although downbeat became his most successful album to date, boasting a stream of Top 3 singles. A dark spate of personal tragedy tinged the songs and by baring his soul, George gained respect from critics who had previously derided his work.

Stating 'I'd rather write a song about my private life than talk about it' George soon became known as an instinctive musician who is meticulous to the point of perfection.

George has always enjoyed collaborating with other high-profile artists and performing cover versions of his favourite songs, to the extent of dedicating an entire tour to performing other writers' work in 1991. The Miscellaneous section in this book is devoted to the subsequent releases of George's duets and covers, among other anomalies.

At present George is concentrating on his own recently formed record label, Aegean, which is fast becoming a leading force in the expanding world of the Internet. His impending solo *Greatest Hits* package is, at the time of writing, planned for release in late 1998 and will no doubt include some form of interactive element, in addition to the rumoured 22 hit singles and three or four new tracks. George is also the first popular singer / songwriter to limit his fan-club exclusively to the Internet.

Atomic has found the following books invaluable: *Bare* by George Michael & Tony Parsons, *George Michael – The Making of a Superstar* by Bruce Dessau and *Wham! The Death of a Supergroup* by Johnny Rogan. Atomic would like to thank Frankie for his computer, Elton for his alias, Deborah Harry, Chris Charlesworth and J B Ward & Son.

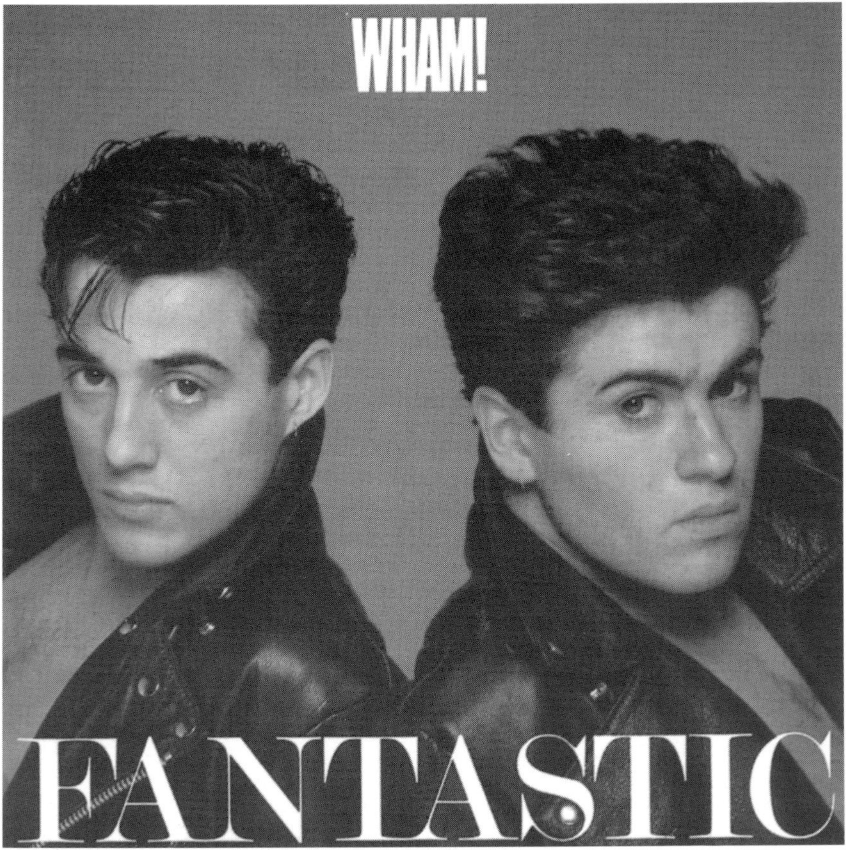
WHAM!
FANTASTIC

FANTASTIC

(ORIGINAL UK RELEASE: INNERVISION IVL 25328, RELEASED JULY 1983
CURRENT CD: EPIC EPC 450090 2)

Having achieved their dream of signing a record contract with Innervision (a subsidiary of CBS), George Michael and Andrew Ridgeley set about recording their début album in the spring of 1982. Rapidly George began to realise the enormity of the task ahead, as the personnel at the infant label had no more idea of the process than the two teenage boys they had signed, just one day after forming the company. 'The record industry is a bunch of headless chickens; they couldn't tell me what to do because they didn't know themselves,' observed George in his 1990 autobiography *Bare*.

'Wham! Rap' was the first of their original demos to be recorded and was produced by Bob Carter. On the strength of his production of Junior's 'Mama Used to Say', Wham! chose Carter in the hope of emulating a similar blend of rock and pop. Unhappy that the resulting sound was not 'black' enough, George went on to co-produce the rest of the album with Steve Brown of ABC fame. Steve introduced the boys to bass player Deon Estus, who in turn brought his drummer Trevor Morrell to join accomplished session musician Anne Dudley, later of the Art of Noise. Andrew Ridgeley shared guitar duties with the much respected Robert Ahwai.

Meanwhile 'Wham! Rap', the band's vibrant first single, was released in June 1982 to little public interest. Nevertheless, the boys doggedly pursued their image by making numerous appearances at London's trendiest night spots, miming and dancing to their music. The producer of the wacky children's TV programme *Swap Shop* was so impressed by one such performance at Stringfellows that he invited the dynamic duo to appear on the show. This was shortly followed by their début appearance on *Top Of The Pops* to promote their second stab at chart success, 'Young Guns'. The timing of this particular invitation was uncanny, as problems with distribution had almost turned fatal with the single literally selling out at the vital position of Number 24 – *Top Of The Pops* proved to be just the boost Wham! needed to propel the track to Number 2. Not long after this success, 'Wham! Rap' was re-released and 'Bad Boys' completed the trilogy of youthful unrest.

After a year and a half of preparation, *Fantastic*, dedicated to two late school chums Andrew Leaver and Paul Atkins, was finally released to great teenage anticipation, entering the charts at Number 1. By now Wham! had a loyal following, despite the dubious critics who were preoccupied with the issue of whether or not the boys' overall message was a parody. Regardless, *Fantastic* feels strangely empty, partly because it contains only eight songs, four of which were singles and one a cover version. There is also a certain lack of continuity between tracks, and while most of the songs are fresh and lively, the overall

feeling remains one of immaturity, moreover, inexperience. It was almost certainly Wham!'s good looks and slightly subversive image that sold the record, rather than any serious signs of songwriting talent at this stage.

Bad Boys
(George Michael)

'Whoo-Hoo!' shriek our boys in leather, as they instantly propel us into their world of teenage rebellion and laddish hedonism. Whilst being a fresh and engaging opener on the album, this song was at the time the third Wham! single in a row to champion the 'soul boy – dole boy' lifestyle that had become synonymous with the group, and it was wearing more than a little thin. George himself was wary of falling into a creative cul-de-sac as he uncharacteristically laboured for three months over this rather simplistic, standard pop song, which merely regurgitated the previously successful formula. By cockily and somewhat unwisely informing us that he is now 'nineteen, handsome, tall

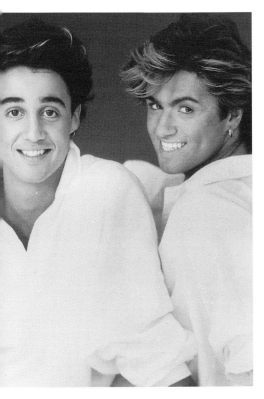

and strong', it comes as little surprise that George later admitted that 'Bad Boys' was the 'lowest point' in the band's career and certainly an image George would fight to relinquish in his later solo years.

A Ray Of Sunshine
(George Michael)

Assuming his best falsetto Bee Gees voice, George churns out this catchy pastiche of Seventies disco pop which exposes his and Andrew's shared passion of dancing the night away, *Saturday Night Fever* style: 'Without this beat my life would fall apart'. Featuring an infectious guitar riff, hand claps and classic disco percussion, this is pure good-time music, despite its intensely off-putting female refrain, 'Watch out boy'. Although it does not particularly stand out as a work of genius, 'A Ray Of Sunshine' sustains the fun-loving image of the pair and sits well on the album.

Love Machine
(W. Moore / W. Griffin)

Continuing the disco flavour of the album, 'Love Machine' is a faithful cover of the Miracles' song, which was one of the first records to influence the young George in the Seventies. The musical arrangement, complete with cheesy strings and pounding bass, stays true to the original thus dating the song somewhat. Oddly though, George delivers a surprisingly disappointing vocal which is so lacklustre in emotional definition that it doesn't even sound like him. Apart from the same suggestive grunt, he makes little use of the potentially incendiary lyrics, which revolve around sex and electricity. George however, was particularly pleased with his interpretation, arrogantly proclaiming that there was 'no way I could have done it better!' This short but fun cover healthily promotes the boys' clubbing image, and was fully supported by a frantic dance routine and far superior rendition on the popular Eighties music programme, *The Tube*.

Wham! Rap (Enjoy What You Do?)
(George Michael / Andrew Ridgeley)

Perfectly capturing the essence of the early Wham! aesthetic, this eponymous rap gloriously and controversially encouraged the post-Falklands War youth to collectively stick two fingers up at the Thatcherite establishment. Whilst the boys were heavily criticised for openly endorsing the pleasures of life on the dole, on another level the double-edged lyrics positively advocate rising above the stigma of unemployment.

Effortlessly mixing his pop and soul roots, George simultaneously celebrates and satirises the then world-wide phenomenon of rap. In the same vein as the massive Trevor Horn production on rival groups like Frankie Goes To Hollywood, the arrangement features a hard-hitting bass, funky guitar, sparkling piano chords and the ubiquitous hand claps, culminating in a powerful backing that flourishes at the end of an incessantly busy vocal. This precocious piece of pop reaches its climax with a chorus of imitative audience participation. Wham! Bam!

Club Tropicana
(George Michael / Andrew Ridgeley)

Cashing in on their suave Mediterranean looks, our boys from Bushey antagonised critics by trading in their giros for a Yuppie holiday in the tropics. 'Club Tropicana', Wham!'s fourth hit single released at the same time as the album, provided the perfect soundtrack to the long hot summer of 1983, and posters of the deeply sun-tanned duo adorned the walls of every lustful pre-pubescent from here to Hertfordshire. The evocative chirping of crickets and the revving of engines entice us into a swanky cocktail bar where George is greeted personally and welcomed to the party. His smooth vocals undulate over a rippling piano set against a lilting bossa nova beat, tropical sounding horns and carnival percussion, conjuring up a carefree yet highly sophisticated atmosphere. Although

widely panned for the drastic change of image, this smoochy number was refreshing in its novelty and proved a welcome showcase for George's previously underexposed singing ability.

Nothing Looks The Same In The Light
(George Michael)

This insipid and painfully immature filler reflects George's well-known early lack of confidence in his looks and personality as we are forced to share with him the night he first becomes a man. George, having successfully completed his manly conquest, lies awestruck next to his more accomplished lover, terrified of the moment she awakes lest she should find him unattractive and regret her actions; 'Please be kind, don't change your mind'. What should be endearing becomes repelling as the thoroughly irritating whisper of a vocal and hugely unsubtle and unsuitable synth line only serve to highlight his inexperience.

On the positive side, within the security of the album George is able to experiment

in playing most of the instruments himself. However it would appear at this stage that George's aplomb disappears with Andrew, whose egocentric presence is glaring in its absence.

Come On!
(George Michael)

Notable only for its appearance on an early demo, this largely disposable pop song attempts to recapture the party spirit and thumping bass of 'Club Tropicana', but unfortunately falls flat with its lifeless repetition of an instantly forgettable tune and meaningless lyrics. The horns, strong throughout the album, provide the track's sole saving grace.

Young Guns (Go For It!)
(George Michael)

This anti-marriage battle-of-the-sexes rap effectively predates the current TV series Men Behaving Badly by about a decade! Wham!'s first successful single scored instantly with the radio stations, soon achieving Top 3 status after a

camp, finely choreographed Top Of The Pops appearance, which introduced an early incarnation of girlie backing duo Shirlie Holliman and D C Lee (later to replaced by Pepsi De Marque). Not only could most teenagers easily relate to the idea of a girl coming in between best mates ('Death by matrimony!'), but they were also able to adopt the dance routine when the song was played in discos. The amusing and vivacious lyrics blend seamlessly with a clean mix of funk and lightweight pop, climaxing in a vigorous, almost playground-like confrontation, punctuated by snappy horns. A well deserved hit.

INSTRUMENTAL
REMIXES

To promote the newly introduced format of the Compact Disc and cassette rather than vinyl, Wham! added three bonus tracks of instrumental remixes to Fantastic (widely available except in North America).

Annoyingly, they are placed in a way that interrupts the intended running order of the original album; thus 'A Ray Of Sunshine' and 'Love Machine' are repeated in sequence after just one track, and the Les Dawson-esque piano bust-up loses its jokey afterthought effect when followed by the instrumental remix of 'Nothing Looks The Same In The Light'. Apart from increasing the length of the album it remains a mystery why George endorsed these tracks as they certainly detract from Wham!'s début as a whole.

A Ray Of Sunshine (Instrumental Remix)
(George Michael)

The instrumental remix of this track adds little of new musical interest, but noticeably removes the solid drumbeat and enthusiastic vocals which had spurred the original on. This unnecesary rehash obviously sickens the lads so much that they feel the need to throw up at the end!

Love Machine (Instrumental Remix)
(W. Moore / W. Griffin)

Straying just a little further away from Wham!'s cover version, this remix replaces the weak vocals of the verses with sickly sweet Seventies strings and rightly places emphasis on the more substantial choruses. A splendidly over-the-top breakdown of drums set against vocals at the end sees the band joyfully letting their hair down and eventually succeeds in dragging the music into the Eighties. The best of a bad bunch by far.

Nothing Looks The Same In The Light (Instrumental Remix)
(George Michael)

Again? Must we?

WHAM!

MAKE IT BIG

MAKE IT BIG

(EPIC EPC 86311 / COLUMBIA 39595, RELEASED NOVEMBER 1984
CURRENT CD: EPIC EPC 465576 2)

Following the expensive dissolution of their contract with Innervision and a court case fighting for ownership of their name, Wham! were saved from financial disaster when CBS re-signed them to another of their subsidiaries, Epic. This fresh start gave them a cash injection sufficient to spend six weeks recording their second album in the sunny South of France. Wham! could now afford the luxury of the prestigious Chateau Minerval studios previously favoured by the likes of Pink Floyd, Yes and Duran Duran. The result was the arrogantly, and rather accurately titled *Make It Big* follow-up album which saw the boys, now in their twenties, fronting an unexpected change of image. In total contrast to the shoe-string budget cover shots of *Fantastic*, George and Andrew had metamorphosed into Armani-suited, seductively pouting and immaculately coiffed heart-throbs, albeit of the squeaky clean variety.

During the recording of *Make It Big* the boys were thrilled to meet their childhood hero Elton John, with whom George was to form a long lasting friendship and a profitable future working relationship. Wham! were by now becoming accustomed to mixing in celebrity circles, and their status was bolstered with a massive £10,000 launch party at the Xenon nightclub in London. This carefully orchestrated event drew enough glittering stars, including such chart competition as members of Spandau Ballet and Duran Duran, to keep the paparazzi flocking for hours. The fervent promotion continued with a demanding tour which firmly established them world-wide, and they notably returned twice to the United States following their smash hit with 'Everything She Wants'.

Make It Big has a distinctive Sixties flavour both musically and lyrically. Having written most of the songs, George's presence is dominant as he acts as sole producer and arranger. He also gains the confidence to unleash his exceptional vocal ability as well as playing many of the keyboards and assuming all backing duties. The album, lauded by George to be 'ten times better than the first one' is a slick affair, unquestionably more mature and self-assured than their début, though unavoidably not as fresh. However there is a strangely familiar hollowness to their second attempt, not least because once again there are only eight songs; four of which were hit singles and one a Motown cover!

Despite not achieving full critical and artistic success, the duo flourished in the charts as a singles band and the Number 1s began to flow thick and fast. Wham! symbolised an entertaining pop music era, battling against such established heavyweights as Culture Club and Frankie Goes to Hollywood, and sparking off a much publicised designer T-shirt war with the latter: for 'Frankie Says Relax', read 'Choose Wham!' Nevertheless, in spite of the overall impression of Eighties optimism, the cracks were beginning to show. Incongruously tacked onto the end of a Wham! album was George's first solo

single 'Careless Whisper', for which he was the youngest ever winner of the Ivor Novello Songwriter of the Year Award in 1985, at the mere age of 21.

Wake Me Up Before You Go-Go
(George Michael)

Famously inspired by a misspelt note from Andrew, 'Wake Me Up Before You Go-Go' rapidly became one of the best-loved Wham! releases, quite possibly because it was 'that much more stupid than anything else!' as George himself later remarked. 'Go-Go' procured the group's first major chart success and it was this Number 1 hit that really broke Wham! in the United States. George particularly revelled in volleying typically American music straight back to the Americans. From the very first 'Jitterbug', Wham! produce a sleek, well crafted piece of pristine pop which is a million miles from the juvenile whooping and bragging as heard on *Fantastic*.

The most striking transformation is the confidence that George demonstrates with the enormous strength of his vocal delivery; gone are the days of rap, replaced with a maturity that was to become one of the most remarkable voices in the industry. This polished jive confection introduces the predominantly nostalgic theme to the album, mixing lyrical references to Doris Day and Jitterbugging with frivolous 'boom-boom's and 'bang-bang's to irresistible effect. The great beauty of this track is that it doesn't aspire to be anything more than pure pop, yet it attains its goal magnificently.

Everything She Wants
(George Michael)

Marking an important development in George's songwriting ability, 'Everything She Wants' retains the accessibility and vocal range of 'Go-Go' whilst dealing with a significantly deeper subject matter. George once again takes full control, playing the idiosyncratic splashy keyboard parts and harmonising with himself in a sorry tale of being trapped in an unhappy marriage: he is the sole breadwinner whose pecuniary efforts never suffice; 'If my best isn't good enough / then how can it be good enough for two?' A repetitive

and static backing intuitively reflects the frustration within the stagnant marital predicament, while George emotes his desperation with a poignant vocal. This stylish track is reminiscent of Michael Jackson's early solo material, and was remixed and released in the UK as a double A-side single with 'Last Christmas' – come Boxing Day DJs were instructed to flip the festive ditty to its darker half.

Heartbeat
(George Michael)

This truly dreadful Sixties pastiche suffers from an overblown piano rendition, ghastly castanets, melodramatic vocals and a serious loss of credibility. Wailing theatrical lines such as 'How could I help but admire her beauty / Standing on the line between desire and duty', 'Heartbeat' would be more fitting on a West End hybrid of *Grease* and *The Rocky Horror Picture Show*. Thus began the unfortunate Barry Mannilow comparisons!

Like A Baby
(George Michael)

Providing another outlet for George's solo musings, this track is a welcome break from the brash unsubtlety of 'Heartbeat' with a surprising two full minutes of lilting instrumental before the entry of the vocals. Sadly the novelty soon wanes as the music is unfortunately exposed as being no more than easy listening, mid-Atlantic muzak and George's exceptionally mannered crooning contains little of substance. This smoochy, late-night number is pleasant enough to doze off to, and Barry Manilow lives on.

Freedom
(George Michael)

Wham!'s grandeur returns with the mighty 'Freedom' anthem, blasting out instantly recognisable brass power chords and blowing the cobwebs left from the previous two tracks clean away. Incredibly written in a taxi en route to the recording studios in France, and completed within 24 hours, this classic crowd pleaser is full of energetic optimism and suitably continued Wham!'s string of Number 1s. Reinforcing their new clean-cut image, the boys promote their preference of fidelity within an open relationship; 'I don't want your freedom / I don't want to play around'. George's stunning falsetto literally pounds over a virtuoso piano and a Sixties beat, fully restoring the wholesome vitality of 'Go-Go'.

If You Were There
(The Isley Brothers)

Opening with a rather fetching hook, this winsome Isley Brothers cover arguably stands out as the album's only non-single that is worthwhile. During one of the most genuine moments on *Make It Big*, Wham! gracefully master the easy accessibility of the Jackson Five appeal with sweet soul vocals and a finger-clickin'-good accompaniment. With this unpretentious and mellow rendition, the boys pay a thoughtful and respectful homage to the best of Seventies Motown.

Credit Card Baby
(George Michael)

This lesser version of 'Go-Go' rudely dispels the geniality left by 'If You Were There' with the kind of trashy brass intro so fully exploited by Huey Lewis and the News throughout the Eighties. Hardly stretching his songwriting skills, George sticks with the middle-of-the-road American feel and comes up with a vaguely toe-tapping filler, but injects none of his characteristic spark or momentum. By now the well established goody-goody image has reached saturation point, and even the amusingly coy narrative of a gold-digger's quest to win her man does not save the song from being little more than irritating, and quite frankly tacky candyfloss.

Careless Whisper
(George Michael / Andrew Ridgeley)

No self-respecting George Michael fan would be without this timeless ballad, featuring perhaps the most famous sax line ever written, and responsible for more slow dance smooches than any other. This solo George Michael single became Epic's first million seller, reaching Number 1 the world over, and has consistently topped polls of the public's favourite songs ever since. George had originally travelled to the Muscle Shoals studios in Alabama to record this song with the legendary soul producer, Jerry Wexler. On his return George felt unhappy with the impersonal result and eventually re-recorded it himself with Andy Richards on keyboards and Steve Gregory on saxophone.

Although unable to completely escape the natural ageing process of all pop songs, 'Careless Whisper' remains one of the most haunting melodies of contemporary music with its lilting acoustic guitar, breathtaking sax and emotionally charged vocals. Ironically George was disappointed that his lyric of infidelity and guilt had such a moving impact as it was one of the first songs he ever wrote, at the tender age of 16, rather flippantly and unromantically on the bus to Bushey! Another paradox is that while Andrew Ridgeley is credited with co-writing 'Careless Whisper', this early Wham! demo effectively sealed his artistic fate, as it also spectacularly formed the ground work to George's solo career.

WHAM!

COMPACT
disc
DIGITAL AUDIO
DIGITALLY MASTERED/ANALOG RECORDING

MUSIC FROM THE EDGE OF HEAVEN

(COLUMBIA CK 40285, RELEASED JULY 1986)

Following the commercial success of *Make It Big*, Wham! sought a unique promotional idea to cement their status, and manager Simon Napier-Bell provided a challenging solution by suggesting they became the first Western pop group to perform in China. This well publicised visit led on to an American invasion of unprecedented proportions; instead of a gruelling Statewise tour, the band pulled off eight stadium shows with a 40,000 strong audience for each performance. Maybe this was the reason why Wham!'s third and final album release in the States was *Music From The Edge Of Heaven*, whereas the UK and the rest of the world were treated to *The Final*; a collection of their greatest hits and highlights from the American album. Due to popular demand *Music From The Edge Of Heaven* is now widely available as an import.

Curiously neither of the above releases sported the traditional glossy pictures of previous Wham! paraphernalia and instead, the cover of *Music From The Edge Of Heaven* boasts a muted photograph of the spectrum taken by Trevor Key, with a rather pensive shot of George and Andrew on the inside. Significantly, each song is marked with the date it was recorded, thus separating 1984's 'Last Christmas' from the current four track EP, *The Edge Of Heaven*. This distinction, added to the lack of unity on the album, prompts the overall impression of a collection rather than a planned release.

Unsurprisingly, Wham! had undergone yet another extreme image transformation and this filtered through to their lyrics; no longer were the boys squeaky clean heart-throbs, they were now super studs singing raunchy songs almost exclusively about sex. Musically pushing their typically bouncy formula to the limit, George instinctively knew how to capitalise on their continued string of Number 1s, and the majority of the eight songs on the album hit the top of the charts world-wide as single releases. Nevertheless, *Music From The Edge Of Heaven* remains a queer hotchpotch of lusty funk, misinformed mixes and sultry ballads.

In preparation for his solo career, it is evident that George had been drawing upon different musical influences for inspiration. This is particularly apparent in the track 'Battlestations' where he adopts the distinctive style of the artist known at the time as Prince. George later proclaimed 'Battlestations' to be his favourite song on the record. In fact, it was obvious that he was changing direction in all aspects of his career, with his experimentation in different musical genres, his outstanding live performance in 'Blue' and the inclusion of his second solo single 'A Different Corner'. By now, George had acquired the very charisma that Andrew Ridgeley had initially contributed to Wham! and the latter's pres-

ence as a stalwart was no longer required.

Whilst George was slaving away in the studio, Andrew suffered an increasing loss of face as he was consistently ridiculed in the tabloid press. The uneasy situation came to a head when George discovered Nomis' imminent take-over by the Kunick Leisure Group, thus associating Wham! with the company that owns the racially notorious Sun City in South Africa. During an interview on the chat show *Aspel & Co.*, George confirmed the rumours of his split from both Nomis and Wham!. Although the break-up was pretty much a foregone conclusion, the ill-fated Andrew was not to learn of his partner's decision until the following day, when he was interrogated by a news-hungry journalist.

The boys parted company amicably at the height of their dazzling career; the *Edge Of Heaven* EP was riding high in the charts as Wham! staged a spectacular farewell concert entitled 'The Final'. In the scorching heat of 28th June 1986 they said their goodbyes at Wembley Stadium in front of 72,000 sweltering and overemotional fans.

The Edge Of Heaven
(George Michael)

Shooting straight to Number 1, Wham!'s incredible parting shot, 'The Edge Of Heaven' ensured that the boys bid farewell with a typically upbeat climax. In this X-rated version of 'Go-Go' the sexual connotations are deliberate, but somehow managed to pass the BBC's censors as they are virtually incomprehensible; 'I would strap you up ...You know I wouldn't hurt you / unless you wanted me to'. George perceptively remarked in his autobiography that 'nobody is going to care because no-one listens to a Wham! lyric; it had got to that stage'. The 'Go-Go' comparisons are considerable, from the catchy barber shop introduction through to the classic banality of the 'Yeah Yeah Yeah' mantra and the sheer exuberance of the frenzied, pounding backing. The vocal melody is also not a million miles away from that of 'Freedom' – a brilliantly simplistic stepwise tune that is instantly appealing and memorable. This track notably features Elton John guesting on piano and the lads' childhood friend, former Executive colleague and later collaborator, David Mortimer (now known as David Austin) on guitar.

Battlestations
(George Michael)

George's fascination with Prince is introduced in this exceptional genuflection including perfectly controlled harmonies and muttered vocal, '1999' drumbeat and poppy keyboard chords. Deon Estus' funky bass provides a solid backbone throughout. Also particularly noteworthy is Rick Taylor's candid trombone solo in contrast to the electronic backing, which was an idea that George explored more fully a decade later in the song 'Older'. Experimenting with new forms of narrative, George resignedly speaks his mind onto his lover's answering machine; 'Why lie to my face / when you can buy a tape machine / to give me bullshit in your place'. Recalling the downbeat mood of 'Everything She

Wants' the brooding vocal is delivered over a repetitive loop with occasional outbursts of stark frustration. Although certain sections of the song fall slightly short of their intended goal, 'Battlestations' is an interesting change in musical direction for George and more than paves the way for his first solo album, *Faith*.

I'm Your Man
(George Michael)

Initiating a pair of heavily remixed Wham! favourites, this eight-minute version of 'I'm Your Man' unfortunately starts with a severely dated and daft introduction. Painfully massacred samples of George's original vocal are set against the sound of Andrew crashing in a car race, only to be met by manic laughter: 'He's brave! He's tough! / Mr Ridgeley, do your stuff!' It soon recovers however into the well-known and famously promiscuous stomping song, which can be found on the compilation album, *The Final*. George vocally as well as lyrically drops all his

inhibitions in this raunchy number which was dashed off during an internal flight on the US tour, and was rumoured to be inspired by his then girlfriend, Brooke Shields. The music is just as explosive and insistent as the lyric, with Deon Estus' impressive bass solo bubbling into the limelight, unfortunately not found on the seven inch release. Try not tapping your toes to this one!

Wham! Rap '86
(George Michael / Andrew Ridgeley)

In the same year as The Police enjoyed renewed success with their farewell mix of 'Don't Stand So Close To Me '86', Wham! chose to remix their début track 'Wham! Rap'. George's new rendition gives the track a harder edge which lends itself appropriately to the more adult album, but noticeably he now strains to reach the notes he sailed through as a teenager, and ironically the outcome is more immature due to the crude sampling of snippets of vocals and the dated Eighties disco beat. Not as fresh and as bright as the original, this version is simply

too long and cringemaking, although the boys' previously expurgated lyrics finally make the cut; 'Don't take no shit from the benefit!' Interestingly neither of the two remixes made it onto *The Final*, thus making them highly desirable collectors' items for their non-American fans.

A Different Corner
(George Michael)

Openly admitting that this song was his first truly autobiographical work, George Michael released 'A Different Corner' as his second solo single (although in the States it was technically his first, 'Careless Whisper' having been attributed to 'Wham! featuring George Michael'). Following an ethereal orchestral introduction, the famous synth line (resurfacing in a similar guise a few years later as the theme music to the cult TV series *Twin Peaks*), instils a mood of serenity and a blank canvas for George's exorcism of his recently lost love. Sounding alternately detached and overwrought, his vocals are tender yet powerful, with the icy cold, delicately simplistic piano recalling the tranquillity of Erik Satie's 'Gymnopédies'. Recorded in Paris, 'A Different Corner' was reputedly the first Number 1 to be written, arranged, produced, performed and sung by the same person. The timing of this release was significant as just prior to this eerily introspective track topping the charts in April 1986, George had officially announced his split with both Wham! and their management.

Blue (Live In China)
(George Michael)

The only live track ever to be released by Wham!, 'Blue', captured on their Chinese Tour, is an exceptionally clean recording thanks to the enforced respect and restraint of the audience. George introduces the performance as being 'very personal to me', which is peculiar, directly following the obvious intimacy of 'A Different Corner'. The song, and in particular the arrangement, appears to be little more than a vehicle to demonstrate George's compelling vocal command. However, the strength of his voice is let down by a disappointingly weak, bass-heavy backing, with shadows of Prince reappearing on the monotonous keyboards and Andrew's less than tuneful guitar effort tellingly low in the mix. The rather unbecoming melody seems to have no ultimate direction, and haplessly seems to mirror the drone of 'Nothing Looks The Same In The Light'.

Where Did Your Heart Go?
(Don Was / David Was)

Wham!'s obligatory cover version on this album is of Was (Not Was)'s rather rambling ballad, 'Where Did Your Heart Go?' This was an unusual choice for George as it was a virtually unknown song by the Detroit based funk group, who were not to find fame themselves until the late Eighties, with the likes of their hit 'Walk The Dinosaur'. Neither the music nor the lyrics are particularly in keeping with Wham!'s present racy style; only Andy Hamilton's moody sax break vaguely hints at their own creative input. After a hauntingly evocative intro, the track rapidly descends into a quagmire of impassioned wailing and shapeless, flat accompaniment. Despite the pseudo sophistication of the seductive late-night atmosphere, this cover is tame and repetitive with an ugly and unsingable chorus.

Last Christmas
(George Michael)

In a typically shrewd piece of forward planning, George ensured with the release of 'Last Christmas' that his dulcet tones would be heard every Yuletide from 1984 to eternity. However it was the first single to sell over a million yet not reach Number 1, kept off at the time by a little thing called Band Aid. In a generous move, Wham! decided to donate all the royalties from sales of 'Last Christmas' to the same cause as the above fundraiser; aiding relief workers during the famine in Ethiopia. Written during the same quiet period as 'Wake Me Up Before You Go-Go', this perennial favourite is conspicuous at the conclusion of Wham!'s last album, and would have sat more comfortably against the more

pertinent backdrop of the *Make It Big* album released earlier that year. After an extended introduction of woeful keyboards, the famously chugging chorus kicks in, soon to be joined by festive sleigh bells. Whilst earlier on 'Heaven' George's lyrics have been X-rated, they are now strictly PG as he warbles easy pop emotion about a sugar coated heartbreak the previous Christmas. Although intensely singable, the music is an irritating carillon pushed along by overpowering drum programming. This extra long version endlessly repeats the chorus well into Boxing Day. Delightful.

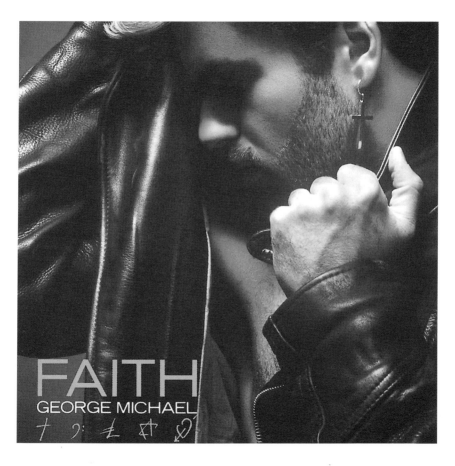

FAITH

(EPIC EPC 460000 2 / COLUMBIA 40867, RELEASED NOVEMBER 1987)

Having tentatively tested the water with the Aretha Franklin duet, 'I Knew You Were Waiting (For Me)', George felt that he had established his personality firmly enough to unleash an entire solo album upon his ever expanding audience. At the conclusion of Wham! George had slumped into a deep, soul searching depression as he contemplated his future musical career. Consequently, the underlying stimulus for the album *Faith* is this personal catharsis, as he readily admits on the cover dedication: 'These songs are the result of the last two years of my life'.

Unsurprisingly *Faith* is written, arranged and produced by George. Cleverly constructed to attract strong American interest, *Faith* fully attained its aspirations by producing six hit singles and achieving the longest ever period at Number 1 in the US charts by a British solo artist. *Faith* also scooped Best Album at the prestigious Grammy Awards and the title track won George his second Ivor Novello Songwriting Award. Proving its universal appeal even further and causing bitter polemic remarks from certain artistic camps, *Faith* became the first album in ten years by a white act to reach Number 1 in the American Black Albums chart – ironically, the antecedent had been George's idols the Bee Gees a decade earlier, with Wham!'s beloved *Saturday Night Fever*. Back on his home turf, *Faith* entered the UK charts at Number 1 and stubbornly resided in the Top 100 for a mammoth 72 weeks. World-wide sales reached upwards of 15 million.

Rather than being of religious significance, the title *Faith* related more to George's growing conviction in himself; 'because before that period of my life, there had been a lack of it'. However, in the same way that Madonna concurrently utilised her Catholicism to spark controversy with the album *Like A Prayer*, George was not adverse to sporting crucifix earrings during his erotic videos. This pseudo religious trademark also appeared on the cover photograph, where George perhaps takes the theme of self-examination to the extreme in checking himself for bodily odour! Whatever the true intention of this picture, it is interesting to note that at this stage in his career George chose to market himself as a sex symbol, recognising once again that his leather clad, designer-stubbled good looks could take him one stage further in reaching a mass market.

Accompanying George on the cover sleeve are symbols representing the five most important things in his life; music, money, love, faith and religion.

This pivotal release mopped up the massive boom in the newlyweds market; the teenage Wham!-sters had by now transformed into rich and upwardly mobile twenty-somethings, and George was quickly entrenched as the Yuppie of Pop. Meeting with instant fan adulation and somewhat mixed critical reviews at the time, *Faith* prevails above all as an upbeat dance album, replacing the bouncy exuberance of the days of Wham! with a

more adult and professional funk. The first half of the collection demonstrates more diversity, depth and potential than anything released during the Wham! era, and auspiciously cements the new direction of the George Michael sound. George almost makes it look too easy as he effortlessly emulates assorted musical genres – he famously retorted to *Rolling Stone* in 1988; 'If you can listen to this album and not like anything on it, then you do not like pop music'.

Faith
(George Michael)

Making it eternally difficult to judge which volume to set the stereo on, George Michael formally commences his solo career with Chris Cameron's subdued cathedral organ introduction, recapping the former Wham! glory of 'Freedom'. At the understated climax, the distinctive guitar strumming of 'Faith' kicks in, complimented by a light percussion of finger clicks, tambourine, hi-hats and claps. In essence this is a cheerful rockabilly knock-off, with the repetitive rhythm respectfully mimicking Bo Diddley's box guitar riff and imaginatively capturing the raw Fifties feel of Elvis Presley's Sun Sessions. The story goes that his publisher Dick Leahy had half-heartedly suggested that George should write a rock'n' roll pastiche, and two days later he was promptly, and no doubt smugly presented with the demo for 'Faith'. George went to great lengths however to stress that it was not actually as painless as it appeared, stating; 'You'd be amazed at how much time it takes to be that simple'.

This short but sweet soundbite reached Number 1 in America for four consecutive weeks; it is the apparently effortless ease of the song that is most appealing, intensified by the breathy clarity of the lyrics about choosing chastity when on the rebound. As biographer Tony Parsons astutely remarked; if 'I Want Your Sex' was black, then 'Faith' 'was as white and as happy as an Elvis movie'.

Father Figure
(George Michael)

George's controlled passion continues at a slower pace with this moving ballad revolving around the intimacy between two lovers. Whilst offering protection and support, the lyrics are also subtly suggestive: 'I will be your father figure / Put your tiny hand in mine / I will be your preacher teacher / Anything you have in mind'. George's smouldering vocals are obvious, but nonetheless effective as he glides smoothly from the muted whispery verses to the emotionally lifting choruses. The religious aura initiated by the church organ in 'Faith' is sustained here by the gospel backing harmonies by Shirley Lewis. The music is lent a certain other-worldly quality with the eastern flavoured string pad and its delicacy is enhanced by Hugh Burns' moving guitar solo. 'Father Figure' reached Number 1 in the US for two weeks in February 1988.

I Want Your Sex
(Parts I & II)
(George Michael)

Initially rather crudely titled 'Johnny Sex', 'I Want Your Sex' was originally intended to kick-start his friend David Austin's flagging solo career. Re-thinking his generosity, George saw this as the perfect opportunity to rid himself of his fluffy Wham! image once and for all, by deliberately seeking controversy and, in turn, critical kudos.

Heavily influenced by Prince's light brand of funk, George similarly plays all his own instruments in the first part of this superb shocker. Unsurprisingly, the blatant carnality of this scandalous piece of pop provoked the intended publicity and initially gained George some much needed 'street cred', but unfortunately it backfired as the massive AIDS awareness campaign swept both sides of the Atlantic. George was duly targeted by the more self-righteous critics as promoting promiscuity; 'Sex is natural, sex is good / Not everybody does it, but everybody should'. Despite a hasty re-write of the lyrics to intimate monogamy, the song was still banned by more than a third of American radio stations, dropped by the BBC and restricted from radio play nation-wide before the 9.00 pm watershed. Sales dropped accordingly and for the first time since Band Aid had prevented 'Last Christmas' from reaching the top spot in 1984, a George Michael composition failed to reach Number 1.

Musically speaking, it is not until Part II, 'Brass in Love', that George really begins to swing. Instantly funkier with a walking bass, wah wah guitar and spotlight-stealing horns, this was released as the B-side to the infamous Part I.

One More Try
(George Michael)

Diffusing the brazen sexuality of 'I Want Your Sex', George slows the pace down with a lengthy, contemplative keyboard introduction which gradually evolves into a stately slow waltz . Writing romantic ballads was by now becoming second nature to George and he penned 'One More Try' in just one day, fluently echoing the beseeching and confessional mood of

'Careless Whisper'. This grief-stricken plea complete with angst-laden lyrics is played out to the full, with a soaring falsetto better suited to the territory of crooners like Michael Bolton, and shows George in an amusingly earnest mode as he clings to what little pride he has left after being jilted by a loved one. Get the hankies out!

Hard Day
(George Michael)

The haunting solo synth introduction breaks into a heavy dance rhythm, dominated by a muscular bass line, and a 'Don't bring me down' refrain suggestive of Prince's 'Alphabet Street'. George, staying true to form, plays all the instruments and produces a macho, state-of-the-art piece of techno pop. His lyrics actually amount to no more than yet another sexual conquest, adding a touch of spice with the cleverly sampled vocals giving the unusual impression of male / female interaction. Following a trend pervasive throughout the album, 'Hard Day' bands straight into the next track, thus losing the impact of the desired sharp ending and disturbing the ruminative opening of 'Hand To Mouth'. Intriguingly 'Hard Day' was not released as a single in its own right, yet it became Number 21 in the US R&B charts regardless.

Hand To Mouth
(George Michael)

On the surface 'Hand To Mouth' seems like an innocent peaceful album track with an understated backing, showcasing George's trademark whispery vocals. However, reading between the lines reveals more substance, of an unsettling political nature. George has come a long way from the juvenile stab at authority in 'Wham! Rap', as he now subtly infers his discontent with the current economic climate. George elaborated on his feelings in an interview with the *New York Times*; 'Though there is no doubt that Thatcher has improved Britain's economic status, her ideal has been to make the country a Little America'. He deliberately kept his lyrical references far from obscure; 'There's a big white lady (Margaret Thatcher) / On a big white doorstep (The White House) ; So she ran to the arms of America / And she kissed the powers that be (Ronald Reagan)'. This pensive cut is further illuminated by the tragic prophecy that materialised barely two weeks after the completion of the song. The indiscriminate violence of the first verse was horrifically mirrored by Michael Ryan's rampage through Hungerford, shooting innocent bystanders at random. 'Hand To Mouth' poignantly initiates George's transformation from teeny pop idol to thoughtful, opinionated singer / songwriter.

Look At Your Hands
(George Michael / David Austin)

Tentatively tackling another taboo subject (this time the violence is domestic), George collaborates with his old sparring partner, David Austin, to comment on a real life situation that he had knowledge of; 'Lady look at your hands / You've got two fat children and a drunken man'. Disappointingly, the sloppiness of the musical performance and insistent Wham!-like 'Na na na na na na' vocals combine to provide the album's weakest track, which blends in rather than stands out within such an expressive and diverse assortment of songs. However hard the uncredited brass section and pianist Danny Schogger try, the tune remains lifeless, clumsy and cluttered, and labours its point to the extreme.

Monkey
(George Michael)

Returning to his super-sexy strut whilst retaining his controversial stance on lyrics, George belts out this funky dance track, fully complimented by Robert Ahwai's spiky guitar. Against a driving beat George sings of a partner with a non-specific problem; the lyric's universal appeal allows the subject to be interpreted as a drug dependency, a reappearing ex-lover or a general chip on the shoulder. Whatever the Monkey may be, it is represented musically with synthesised jungle effects and simian screeches.

With its euphoric energy and atmospheric mood changes, 'Monkey' translates well into live performance and George amusingly included a large cage as part of the set during its rendition on the *Faith* tour. In America, George's record label Columbia released a feverish remix by Jimmy Jam and Terry Lewis, who were ex-members of Prince's band The Time and sometime producers of Janet Jackson. Overtly aimed at a black audience, the 'Monkey' remix became the only George Michael single to accomplish Number 1 status in the US club charts until a decade later, when he repeated this success with 'Star People'.

Kissing A Fool
(George Michael)

Originally earmarked as the title track of the album, 'Kissing A Fool' was written in the period before *The Edge Of Heaven* but put to one side with George's indeterminate professional future in mind. The age of the track is uncomfortably evident as it sticks out like a sore thumb within the context of *Faith*, and it would be hard to imagine this anomalous piece heralding George's solo career as intended.

Bruce Dessau observes the uncharacter-istic nature of this song in his biography *George Michael – The Making of a Superstar*, as being 'a shuffling piece of supper club fake jazz that stands up only in terms of its parodic appeal'. Indeed, 'Kissing A Fool' perfectly captures the mood, timing and feel of its intentions in reproducing a smoky Forties ballad, yet however smoothly George asserts his craft, his roots are definitely not in jazz. Despite the authentic walking bass, rhythmic brushes and shuffling beat, this experiment in pastiche almost seems too easy for George and, quite frankly, Harry Connick Jr. does it with more sincerity and style.

Hard Day
(Shep Pettibone Remix)
(George Michael)

Should you become lulled to sleep by the mellow suavity of 'Kissing A Fool', then this dance remix will wake you up with a start! Appearing on the CD version only, George untypically allowed another producer's personality to dominate this bonus track. His choice of remixer was cunningly calculated, as Shep Pettibone was consistently enjoying success with such hip American megastars as Madonna, Janet Jackson and Paula Abdul. Continually influenced by Prince during the recording of *Faith*, George had adopted his diminutive mentor's ploy of sampling and playing back vocals at different speeds to create varying pitches, thus enlarging his vocal range. This technique was exploited to the hilt by Pettibone, who also added a new keyboard part. The 'Hard Day' remix smacks of the dance releases by MC Hammer and Bobby Brown and screams EIGHTIES!

A Last Request
(I Want Your Sex Part III)
(George Michael)

Another bonus track, this time included on both CD and cassette formats, 'A Last Request' completes the 'I Want Your Sex' trilogy with a downbeat, late-night conclusion. Toning down the original drum loop and adding seductively unintrusive muted brass, George hushedly intones what appears on the surface to be a simple, intimate love song but is in fact a rather sinister affair. In 'I Want Your Sex (Monogamy Mix)' George had praised the virtues of a healthy sexual appetite within a steady relationship, 'the only way I was going to get the sex was with consent', but by the end of this unholy trinity George has resorted to a devious plan in order to bed his partner. With the muffled words, 'It's late, time for bed / So I sit and wait / For that gin and tonic to go to your head' we are left with the distinct impression that George is not quite the gentleman he would lead us to believe. Not so much 'A Last Request' as 'A Last Demand' this somewhat Machiavellian design leaves a slightly sour residue after such a monumental album.

LISTEN WITHOUT PREJUDICE VOLUME I

(EPIC EPC 467295 2 / COLUMBIA 46898, RELEASED SEPTEMBER 1990)

Following a gruelling nine month world tour to promote *Faith*, a physically and mentally exhausted George Michael enjoyed a slightly quieter year in 1989. When he was not receiving numerous awards at prestigious ceremonies or being spotted walking his hyperactive Labrador Hippy across Hampstead Heath, George was preparing for his next career move. Ever concerned about popular opinion, he embarked upon redefining his public image once again with the aim of producing an album of mature, thought-provoking songs. Simultaneously George worked on projecting his own point of view via his autobiography *Bare*, written with Tony Parsons, in an attempt to escape the contrived but likeable figure of *Faith* and create an intelligent and artistic portrait of himself. The book was relatively easy as Tony Parsons was a capable and respected Fleet Street journalist who had covered Wham! on many occasions, but the music posed a greater problem as George hit the difficult 'second album' syndrome.

George realised that simply producing 'Faith II' was out of the question and would probably have been disappoining in an artistic sense. However he was confident that whatever he presented would get a decent hearing as a result of the mass audience whipped up by *Faith*. Indeed, his forthcoming project was eagerly anticipated and the precursory period seemed to be besieged by contradicting rumours on the album's length and content. Just six months prior to its release the new collection was officially announced to be a double album, but was changed to a single volume of ballads shortly to be followed by a second half of dance tracks. In September 1990, George's project finally emerged under the guise of *Listen Without Prejudice*, with the intriguing subtitle 'Volume I'.

Referring to the dubious title, George clarified, 'the album should be listened to by all types and all races with an open mind'. Significantly, shortly after being interviewed for *The South Bank Show* by Melvyn Bragg, George made a shock revelation announcing his retirement from the public eye – there would be no more promotion, interviews or videos featuring himself. Marking this departure, George decided not to appear on the front cover of the album, instead choosing an anonymous photograph of 1940s sunbathers. The promo for the first single 'Praying For Time' simply features the lyrics on a black screen, whilst 'Freedom 90' boasts a succession of supermodels lip-synching George's words as his *Faith* jacket is symbolically burnt.

Recorded at Sarm West and Metropolis Studios in London, George's second solo album explores a low-key intimacy that is heightened further by his inclusion of the songs' dates, lending the work an almost diaristic feel. Coupled with the recurring themes of emotional vulnerability and a questionably unctuous social commentary, *Listen* comes across as George's most serious work to date. Sales undoubtedly suffered as a result of poor management in choosing the singles and their release dates – implausibly the album was released just two weeks after the first single, thus quelling the fans' desire for future purchases. Predictably, although the singles maintained an unusually low profile, the album fared far better in the charts; achieving an instant Number 1 in the UK and a respectable Number 2 in the US. Whilst world-wide sales did not scale the heights of *Faith*'s incredible success, *Listen* was regarded by many as undeniable proof of George Michael's artistic legitimacy, winning the BRIT Award for Best British Album in February 1991. An indication of what was hopefully yet to come, George said in one of his 'last' interviews with *The*

Mirror in 1990: 'With other albums I have been exhausted and by the end, glad they were over. With this one, I felt like carrying on and on.'

Praying For Time
(George Michael)

George Michael's opus commences with this anthemic ode to destitution, which is indicative of the overall feel of *Listen Without Prejudice Volume I*. The powerfully majestic production flows bravely across the entire album and the lyrical theme introduces a more mature and worldly-conscientious singer / songwriter. The album's acoustic instrumentation is initiated here with a jangly folk guitar, highlighting a sombre descending chord sequence with a gravitational pull that, along with the strong social message of the song quite literally brings you down to earth.

'Praying For Time' has been widely compared to the style of John Lennon and it is particularly George's vocal that is reminiscent of the late ex-Beatle, as he uses the same close-miked echo made famous by Lennon in his Phil Spector sessions. In true Lennon fashion, George crusades against the desperate plight of today's poverty-stricken society, where the 'open hand' refers to beggars on the street hoping for an occasional guilty gesture; 'charity is a coat you wear twice a year'.

This single became an elected morale booster for US military personnel as they prepared to leave for service in the Gulf War and consequently fared better overseas in terms of chart sales. George pointedly protested against its wartime appeal and like 'Careless Whisper', 'Praying For Time' means more to the grieving masses than it does to its creator, who stated simply, 'The song was just my idea of trying to figure out why it's so hard for people to be good to each other'.

Freedom 90
(George Michael)

As George stated in an interview for *The Mirror* at the time, 'my new single is about how I got away from selling myself because of my looks and got on with what I'm best at and enjoy most – writing songs'. Updating the Wham! hit with the effusive funk more recently heard on *Faith*, 'Freedom 90' provides George with a vehicle to say goodbye to his image conscious past and instil in his listeners some respect for his craft; 'Gotta have some faith in the sound / It's the one good thing that I've got'. The confessional lyrics teamed with a bright and breezy backing that features a famously funky piano riff and a curiously controlled gospel chorus, combine to create this feel good liberation chant.

George adopts a deliberate enthusiasm to reflect the optimistic vigour of his rose tinted memories with Wham! and his hope for the future. Rather ironically, on his departure from the Wham! inspired band, Take That, Robbie Williams covered this song to kickstart his own solo career and fared significantly better than George, whose release of 'Freedom 90' was delegated to 'third single' and consequently made little impression on the charts.

They Won't Go When I Go
(S Wonder / Y Wright)

On first hearing, this is a spine-tingling, hauntingly stark version of Stevie Wonder's spiritual composition. The sightless yet visionary musician was famous for using all the latest technology to create a brand of Seventies black progressive rock and this was typical for his song 'They Won't Go When I Go'. In contrast, for his version, George strips the arrangement to the bare essentials of Chris Cameron's piano and his own emotionally charged vocals. George explained that he felt Stevie Wonder's original was, 'a beautiful song which had not been arranged to full effect... there was so much synth work going on that it detracted from what he was doing as a singer'.

However, upon repeated play, George's melodramatic working of the vocals highlights the unbecoming pomposity of the self-righteous lyrics; 'The greed of man will be / Far away from me / And my soul will be free / They won't go when I go'. Curiously, this social comment is marked in the liner notes as a 'live recording' which is fairly inconceivable considering that although George is multi-talented, it is unlikely that he would have been able to sing more than one part at a time!

Something To Save
(George Michael)

Following the sombre mortality of 'They Won't Go When I Go', 'Something To Save' is instantly lighter on the soul with its bewitching beauty. Penned in December 1988 in bits and pieces at the conclusion of the *Faith* tour, this was the first song written for the new album. George was 'sick to death' of the huge electronic sound supporting

him on stage and chose to write this song on acoustic guitar. He kept it suitably simplistic; 'I thought it had more emotion and clarity without drums, so I kept it to guitars and cellos on the album'. Skilfully weaving an eloquent cello line into the airy arrangement, Emily Burridge and Alfia Nakipbekova later feature on a particularly lucid musical round with Phil Palmer's echoing guitar, which sounds strangely like a sitar. Lyrically, George's self-righteous theme continues but with a simplistic honesty that is far easier to swallow than the preaching of the previous track.

Cowboys And Angels
(George Michael)

Standing at an epic seven minutes in length, 'Cowboys And Angels' was an odd choice for a fifth British release and yet George was disappointed with its lack of commercial success. The moody altered piano introduction is a complete non sequitur as it breaks into a heavy shuffle with George's elastic bass swinging in 6/8 time. Andy Hamilton's surly saxophone, the muffled strings and detached vocals add to the overall cluttered feeling, contrasting with the clarity displayed in earlier tracks. Breaking the chain of George's holier-than-thou sermonising, his lyrics now take on a self-deprecating humility as he helps his partner (ambiguously left gender free:'mister / sister') start afresh after a string of disastrous relationships. Bruce Dessau amusingly quips in his biography *The Making of a Superstar* that George lends this track a 'Sixties film soundtrack feel to make sure his fans didn't OD on despair.'

Waiting For That Day
(George Michael and
Mick Jagger / Keith Richards)

Beginning the slide into commercial oblivion, 'Waiting For That Day' was the second single to be lifted from this album, and only managed to struggle to Number 23 in the UK charts. Opening Side B with the theme of begging for a

fresh start, George welds his carefully constructed samples to direct lyrical and musical quotes from the Rolling Stones' 'You Can't Always Get What You Want'. As explained in great depth in the art and culture documentary *The South Bank Show*, George created the song by first setting up the conflicting groove with a slowed down sample of James Brown's 'Funky Drummer' beat and a Sixties organ purposefully set against a folky guitar riff. Having established this formula, George then wrote the lyrics – an unusual and almost 'backwards' way for him to compose as the lyrics are normally his initial source of inspiration.

Referring to the link with the Stones, George surmised that it was 'just my way of tailing off the song because the song in some sense is about a relationship which has been over but I wanted to rekindle... in the interim neither party had got what they wanted.' George's choice of musical reference perhaps reveals more than he intended, as it betrays the

underlying mood of despondency that suffuses *Listen Without Prejudice*.

Mothers Pride
(George Michael)

By now the constant message of social consciousness is beginning to irk as George's anti-war plea comes across as mawkish and insincere. In order to prove his worth as a profound songwriter, George attempted a poignant tour de force in the style of Bertolt Brecht's *Mother Courage*, evoking the trauma suffered by women through war-time, 'because war and warmongering are always presumed to be male territory'.

Released as a single against George's wishes, this dreary album out-take was generally frowned upon by critics as being an obvious cash-in on the Gulf War. On the other hand radio stations world-wide misconstrued George's pacifistic comment as DJs endorsed it by reading heartfelt messages from the troops to their families over 'Mothers Pride' [sic]. 'I never intended it to be a

single,' George told the *Daily Mirror* in 1993, 'most artists would be respected by their record companies' – a dig which was premonitory of future legal wrangles.

Heal The Pain
(George Michael)

Gaily lifting the depression of 'Mothers Pride', George openly draws from Paul McCartney's school of twee meanderings to produce this cheery piece of easy-going pop. As with the obvious influence of Lennon in 'Praying For Time', George readily admits that this is a well meaning accolade to McCartney as 'Heal The Pain' remains to date 'the most derivative thing I've ever done, but it's such an obvious reference that I don't think anybody would take it as anything other than a tribute.' Engagingly reflective and simplistic, the music is endearingly acoustic with George's honeyed vocals floating over the top with the greatest of ease. George continues to manifest his Beatles-inspired direction here by citing the bossa nova beat recognisable from the *White Album*'s 'I Will'. A jaunty break from the gloom.

Soul Free
(George Michael)

For an artist who has so perfectly mastered the art of dance music, George has recorded disappointingly few dance tracks since the heady days of *Faith* and Wham!. Possibly an indication of the as yet unfulfilled promise of 'Listen Without Prejudice Volume II', the sampled beat of 'Soul Free' crackles into action with a much missed drum sound, and falls leisurely into a reggae dub shuffle. On such an acoustic and downbeat album, the absence of drums and proper dance keyboards is frustrating and the change of instrumentation in 'Soul Free' is a distinctive and welcome dedication to Jazzie B of Soul II Soul fame.

Vocally the carefree George of old has returned as his sexy falsetto conveys the relaxed groove of the song. George was proud of his performance, stating; 'In terms of a vocal it's got the most release on it, it really kind of blasted and I had real fun doing it'. It is a shame that this tune was not released as anything more than a buried B-side, as George could well have avoided the popular criticism that his second solo album was too morbid and depressing.

Waiting (Reprise)
(George Michael)

The musical reference this time for the reprise of 'Waiting For That Day' is not so much Rolling Stones as Bob Dylan. Written four months after its precursor, this snippet is a brief afterthought to the album that explains George's diaristic theme; 'Well, there's one year of my life in these songs / And some of them are about you' along with his current dilemma: 'You look for your dreams in heaven / but what the hell are you supposed to do / when they come true?' The reprise and the album as a whole closes on a positive note as George delivers himself in a long, drawn out vocal climax, asking to be taken at face value as a bona fide songwriter – 'Here I am!'

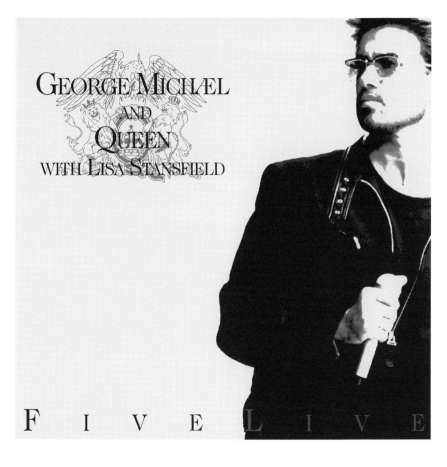

GEORGE MICHAEL AND QUEEN – FIVE LIVE

This extremely successful collaboration between solo star and supergroup was released in two different formats with a separate track listing for the UK and the US, as follows:

UK RELEASE   HOLLYWOOD RECORDS HG 61479, RELEASED APRIL 1993
Track Listing:- Somebody To Love / Killer / Papa Was A Rollin' Stone / These Are The Days Of Our Lives / Calling You / Dear Friends
US RELEASE   PARLOPHONE CDRS 6340, RELEASED APRIL 1993
Track Listing:-39 / These Are The Days Of Our Lives / Somebody To Love /Papa Was A Rollin' Stone – Killer Medley / Calling You

To mark the loss of one of rock's greatest personalities to the rapidly escalating epidemic of AIDS, the three remaining members of the band Queen organised a spectacular concert for their late vocalist, Freddie Mercury. All revenue from this star-studded event at Wembley Stadium and the ensuing EP went to the specially formed Mercury Phoenix Trust, to be distributed to various AIDS charities world-wide. George Michael was one of the privileged members of the rock aristocracy to be invited to contribute to this monumental occasion, and was visibly overwhelmed as Freddie had always been one of his heroes; 'It was probably the proudest moment of my career, because it was me living out a childhood fantasy... to sing one of Freddie's songs in front of 80,000 people.'

George performed three Queen tracks at the concert, 'Somebody To Love', 'These Are The Days Of Our Lives' and '39', which were included on the 'Five Live' EP, along with the innovative 'Killer / Papa Was A Rollin' Stone' medley and 'Calling You', which were recorded during his *Cover To Cover* tour earlier in 1992. This live compilation was the only medium on which George could be heard until the legal battle with his record label Sony was resolved, and it proved to be a smash hit on both sides of the Atlantic. When the marriage of George and Queen was so

well received, expectant rumours circulated that the two mega acts would combine to form a new Queen line-up, but this fantasy alliance sadly never transpired. George's public flattery of his idols was nonetheless wholeheartedly returned by Queen drummer Roger Taylor; 'George Michael's wonderful performance and uncanny vocal resemblance to our much missed Freddie Mercury alone make this project special.'

Somebody To Love
(Freddie Mercury)

Introducing this song as one of his personal favourites, George launches into a superb version of 'Somebody To Love'. In a demanding song for any vocalist, he respectably matches Mercury's soaring tenor, resulting in a much praised highlight of the evening. Graciously managing not to stamp his own personality on the performance, George retains the original drama of the track and passionately does Freddie's emotional plea justice.

Mercury's trademark multi-tracked

vocals are replaced here by the full force of the London Community Gospel Choir and the instrumental backing pays due respect with the obligatory power chords, crashing toms, skidding piano and Brian May's psychedelic guitar solo. The audience adds to the celebratory live atmosphere by participating in a rousing sing-a-long in this, the close of George's set. This rendition translates well into a passionate tribute and is exactly as it should be; a sensational breathtaking climax. George touchingly enthused, 'When I think of Freddie I think of everything he gave me in terms of craft and just to sing those songs, especially 'Somebody To Love', was really an outrageous feeling for me.'

Killer
(Tinley / Seal)

One of the many classics that George chose for his *Cover To Cover* tour was Seal and Adamski's techno anthem, 'Killer', which had reached Number 1 in the UK charts in 1990. Seal was later quoted as being honoured that George covered the song. George had astutely realised that the thumping idiosyncratic bass line could be used as the linking feature between this track and the Grammy winning 1973 Temptations' hit, 'Papa Was A Rollin' Stone'. Starting with the surreal housey keyboard chords of 'Killer', a long and drawn out introduction explores the funky riffs of 'Papa' and creates a huge sense of anticipation. Eventually the recognisable stomp of 'Killer' breaks through to the great delight of the audience, and Seventies meets Nineties in perfect musical fusion. The band stays close to the original, adding just a little extra percussion and while George can't mimic Seal as he can Freddie, he embraces several of Seal's mannerisms and the overall performance is stunning. Sometimes however, George can't help but get lost behind the infectious rhythm which makes it impossible for any listener to stay still! The bass line then seamlessly segues into...

Papa Was A Rollin' Stone
(Norman Whitfield / Barrett Strong)

Recapturing the lengthy instrumental introduction to this medley, 'Papa' is brought in gradually whilst subtly continuing the ubiquitous bass line. George generously donates a verse to each backing singer suggesting great band camaraderie. There are cheers in the audience as he uses this hand-over period to excite the crowd, who perhaps appreciate his dancing a little more than the Motown half of this medley! Although undoubtedly riveting at the time, as the combination approaches nearly twelve minutes in length it sits uncomfortably on a relatively short EP. Returning once again to the pulsating chords of 'Killer' to complete the epic medley, the question is posed whether George is actually commenting on the similarity between the two tracks by default. In order to promote the EP, George supervised but noticeably did not appear in his visually ground-breaking video, where the lyrics were comically interpreted with TV adverts, interspersed with contemporary shots of pierced body parts.

These Are The Days Of Our Lives
(Queen)

Back to the Freddie Mercury tribute concert and George is joined on stage by Rochdale soul sensation Lisa Stansfield for their duet of 'These Are The Days Of Our Lives'. This moving ballad comes as a welcome change from the previous uptempo covers and is an excellent choice for two voices that blend so well in harmony. It is also a nice touch to perform Freddie's swansong as a duet rather than have one superstar overshadow the sentiment of the occasion. The lyrics are lent an added poignancy as Freddie's passing is echoed elsewhere in the concert with Seal's rendition of 'Who Wants To Live Forever'. Queen's original recording of 'These Are The Days Of Our Lives' is transformed into a gorgeous stadium ballad which is understated on an almost supernatural level, and here the sedate, atmospheric backing and

courteous audience allow the vocals to become prominent. Lisa fondly recalled, 'I think I would have to say that was the best day of my life – singing with George... it was obvious that Freddie meant so much to George, so I felt really honoured.'

Calling You
(Bob Telson)

Originally intended as the theme for the film *Baghdad Café*, 'Calling You' was performed by George and Lynn Mabry on the *Cover To Cover* tour and was also depicted in the somewhat tense rehearsal on *The South Bank Show*. Set against a bluesy keyboard accompaniment, the melancholy vocals are somewhat spoilt by the entry of an odiously familiar *Last of the Summer Wine* harmonica theme. Whilst effective on a film soundtrack, this moody number is pretty painful as a live performance and would perhaps have been better suited to the emotional outpourings of *Listen Without Prejudice*.

Dear Friends
(Brian May)

This short and sweet Queen hymn celebrating friendship was first heard on their breakthrough album *Sheer Heart Attack*. Simple and devastatingly effective, Queen's performance of 'Dear Friends' was only included on the UK release of *Five Live*.

39
(Queen)

Not a great song even when performed by Queen, '39' was the B-side to 'You're My Best Friend' and here provides light relief for the audience on a sorrowful occasion. With a sing-a-long and slaphappy Country and Western tune, George remains faithful to Queen's live version with this short and noisy opener to the US release of 'Five Live'. Yee-ha!

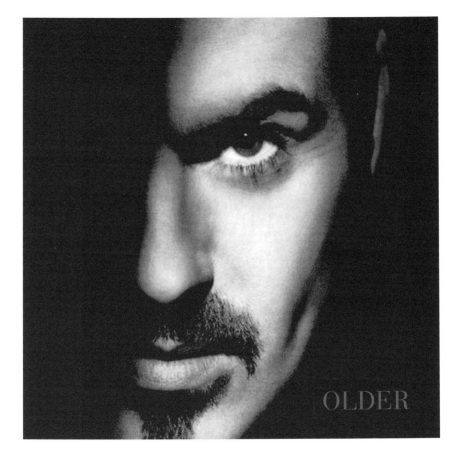

OLDER

OLDER

(AEGEAN / VIRGIN CDV 2802, RELEASED MAY 1996)

After a lengthy and excruciatingly public legal battle with Sony, George was finally extricated from his stifling contract with the aid of a considerable lump sum from Virgin and the newly launched DreamWorks label. More used to dealing in the glossy Hollywood film business, the joint owners Steven Spielberg, Jeffrey Katzenberg and David Geffen looked to expand their empire to incorporate the record industry, and took a gamble by signing the notoriously headline-making George Michael as their premier new act. 'Jesus To A Child' was chosen as their first ever single yet curiously was released halfway through January rather than as expected in time for the Christmas market. However, whilst not particularly forthcoming with the initial release they have since extended *Older*'s life span almost indefinitely.

George dedicated his first album in virtually five years to two influential Brazilians – Antonio Carlos Jobim 'who changed the way I listen to music' and Anselmo Feleppa 'who changed the way that I look at my life'. The former's musical influence is obvious through George's use of rhythm and colour, while George spoke candidly in interviews of the loss of his close friend Anselmo who had been a source of inspiration for the album. In an infamous three part exclusive by Tony Parsons for *The Mirror*, George revealed the extent of his grief and scandalously admitted to smoking 25 cannabis joints a day during the making of *Older*.

Further reflecting his change of attitude towards the media, George started promoting his work once again, complimenting the interviews by recommencing personal appearances in his promo videos, and posing for no less than thirteen photographs on the sleeve of the album. The shots are a good indication to the ensuing content as George is pictured as contemplative and frowning against an arty decor.

Perhaps these pictures constitute another ploy in his ongoing strategy to be taken seriously, whereas with *Listen Without Prejudice Volume I* George had felt that he literally had to become faceless in order to achieve artistic credibility.

Frequently referred to as 'the best Sade album in years', *Older* is a muted collection of smooth late-night ballads, with George's voice rarely rising above a whisper even in the more uptempo tracks. George's vocal restraint is peculiar considering that his self-indulgent lyrics revolve around the unquiet themes of bereavement, misspent years and profound disenchantment. For the first time George's songs occasionally contain a spiteful edge, in particular the waspish 'Star People' and the blatant jibe at Sony in 'Free'. True to form, George assumes the majority of the instrumental duties, which unfortunately translates as suffocating synthesisers, and the sparse flourishes of 'real' instruments are like a breath of fresh air. For those who expected George to

return with a new lease of life after his very public emancipation from his contractual chains, *Older* came as quite a disappointment as its overall impression is saturated by sombre, maudlin self-pity.

Although the tracks on *Older* tend to merge into one long soporific dirge, several songs stand out as exquisite pieces of work when extracted from the overpowering bleakness. Moreover, *Older* has proved to be George's most commercially successful album to date, with all its singles reaching the Top 3 in the UK, compared to *Faith*'s two Top 3 smashes, and *Listen Without Prejudice Volume I*'s measly one Top 10 hit. George's grateful message, 'Thank you for waiting' is perhaps a clue to the success of *Older*, as however much George suffered at the hands of Sony, it is the humble fan, loyally waiting indefinitely for a new album, that is ultimately the injured party.

Jesus To A Child
(George Michael)

With its début performance at the MTV European Music Awards in 1994, 'Jesus To A Child' was George's first new song in three years but was not released until January 1995. The instant Number 1's lush synthesised backdrop, Spanish guitar and powerfully understated vocals exquisitely glide into the sophistication of the album.

The elegiac lyrics have frequently been attributed to the loss of George's gay friend Anselmo Feleppa, who died tragically prematurely of a brain haemorrhage in 1993. George was extensively interviewed in promotion of this single by, among others, Chris Evans on Radio One, Tony Parsons for *The Mirror* and Adrian Devoy for *The Big Issue*, and openly expressed his deep love for the late Brazilian. As he disclosed that many of his songs embrace direct references to his bereavement, 'Jesus To A Child' in particular emerges as one of the most dignified and sensitive ways an artist could 'come out' to his public, especially in light of George's recent enforced revelations. Even George's arch-enemy, ex-manager Simon Napier-Bell, respected the intensely private nature of the song; 'George genuinely appears to be singing only to the person to whom the song is addressed – which leaves the listener feeling like an eavesdropper.' Giving the single a positive double purpose, 'Jesus' was used to raise a total of £50,000 for the charity Help A London Child, with George matching every listener's pledge on a pound for pound basis. Proving even further that George had not lost his touch, the song was awarded Gold Status by the Recording Industry Association just as the follow-up single 'Fastlove' was released.

Fastlove
(George Michael)

Lightening the mood considerably, 'Fastlove' is a funky paean to one night stands, and provides a welcome

glimpse of the hedonistic George of old. Recalling his and Andrew Ridgeley's teenage motto of carefree sex without responsibility, many commented that this sounded almost like a mature version of Wham!, both musically and lyrically. George's only overtly dance track on the album is an impeccable piece of hip-hop which quotes directly from 'Forget Me Nots' by Patrice Rushen. The 1982 hit had been re-recorded by Randy Crawford just a few months before George picked up on its appeal, introducing Jo Bryant singing the catchy 'Forget Me Nots' line. This popular theme song for sex and love addicts with a bump 'n' grind groove is sadly not indicative of the rest of the album, but its lusty inflection and chart-friendly beat ensured its Number 1 placement and earned George the Ivor Novello Award for most performed work in 1996.

Older
(George Michael)

After the traumatic loss felt in the album's opener and the physical need for release expressed in the second song, this reflective title track broaches another prevalent theme of regretting time wasted on meaningless actions. The music is suitably fitting with apocalyptic piano chords and Steve Sidwell's surly muted trumpet, complimented by a surge of vocals soon to dwindle to an unemphatic whisper, as then heard throughout the album. George recognises that he isn't getting any younger and must therefore reshuffle his priorities accordingly: 'These are wasted days without affection / I'm not that foolish anymore'. Along with the realisation that the ageing process even affects pop stars George places his vanity to one side, allowing the cover shot to show his laughter lines without alteration, and voices the wry quip 'Strange / Don't you think I'm looking older?'

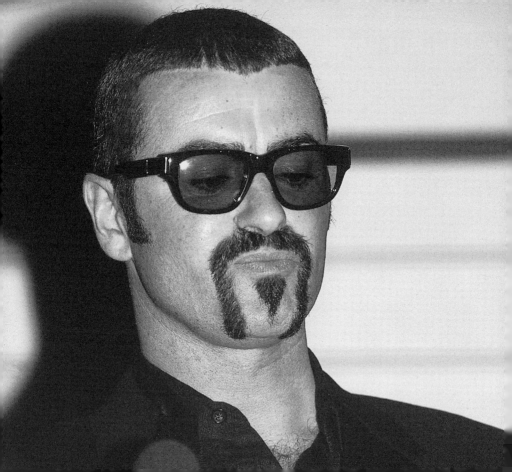

Spinning The Wheel
(George Michael / Jon Douglas)

'Spinning The Wheel' is one of those songs you happily sing along to without realising the full extent of the lyrical connotations. On the surface it is a weary goodbye from a lover who is sick and tired of his philandering partner's night-long escapades, but dig a little deeper and you will discover the miasmic kismet faced by an AIDS generation lover playing a sexual version of Russian roulette. This untraditional male jealousy is anomalous for a commercial pop song in any context, and linked with George's insecurities about his squandered youth and fear of ageing shown previously in *Older*, perhaps points to his nebulous state of mind at the time of recording. Furthermore, the perception displayed in the lyrics and the intimacy with which George sings leaves a feeling of troubled unease. Despite the apprehension of the words, the flawless heavy shuffle and the catchy scratchadelic sample within the unobtrusive music, carried 'Spinning The Wheel' to Number 2.

It Doesn't Really Matter
(George Michael)

George later remarked that 'It Doesn't Really Matter' was 'one of my favourite songs on the album'. Commenting that it was one of the simplest tracks that he had ever recorded, George was pleased with the resulting disparity when he purposefully placed it in the middle of a heavily produced album; 'I love that... but a remarkable number of people don't notice the song'. Lamenting his ambiguous relationship with his father, George designs an uninspiringly languid groove around an antiquated Dr Rhythm box not heard since the early demo days of Wham!. It is little wonder therefore that people do not pay this song much attention as the two-chord music is phlegmatic and George's spaced out vocal line does not rise above a slurred murmur. The sentimental meaning is buried under the chintzy apathy and lethargic mumble, and quite frankly George is capable of fluently recounting an emotive passage with far more piquancy. The title could hardly be more fitting!

The Strangest Thing
(George Michael)

By now the heavily synthesised arrangements combined with George's refusal to sing above a muffled whisper are becoming tedious and repetitive. No matter how personal this song is to George, as he once again deplores his dissipated past and explores his own confused personality, he is unable to evoke empathy from his audience with these detached, hazy ramblings. The constant need for self-assessment is now turning ugly; 'Take my life / Time has been twisting the knife... Take my dreams / Childish and weak at the seams... There's a liar in my head / There's a thief upon my bed'. Overall this is an odd composition coming from George with an uncharacteristically clumsy vocal melody, intensely irritating Japanese Koto sample and inappropriate Turkish vibe. The album is aching for George to loosen up and to either inject some feeling into his vocals or give his fans what he excels at - a lighter-hearted, memorable pop song.

To Be Forgiven
(George Michael)

'To Be Forgiven' is George's most obvious homage to Brazilian composer Antonio Carlos Jobim, which the critic George Varga scathingly described, with justification, as a 'pale attempt to simulate Jobim's understated Brazilian rhythms, urbane lyrics, sultry vocal delivery and harmonically sophisticated arrangements (which) would be laughable if it wasn't so embarrassingly off the mark.' Not even the chromatic flute theme, pastel tinged bossa nova beat or softly picked guitar can detract from the fact that this is Part Two of the self-exploratory theme in 'The Strangest Thing' – although this time he is possibly feeling even more suicidal. The recurrent image of being somehow held down and having to struggle to wake up was expressed in the previous track with the line; 'I cannot seem to get my eyes open' and in 'To Be Forgiven' he is sinking even further into his depression; 'It takes all that I have to cry for help'. George's despair is a strange, questioning one that is impenetrably personal: 'I would beg to be forgiven / If I knew my sin'.

Move On
(George Michael)

Still pondering on his thirty-something crisis, 'I've got to get back on my feet / I feel like I've been sleeping', George thankfully moves into a more positive frame of mind with the help of his 'angel' (presumably Anselmo), who encourages him to pull his life together and stop wasting precious time. The music is suitably upbeat as George invokes the classy jazz club intro of 'Club Tropicana' but elaborates into a grown-up, refined finesse with a smouldering sax and a smooth, undulating vocal. A smattering of applause leads into 'Star People'.

Star People
(George Michael)

Backing singer Jo Bryant's breathy harmonies open this biting attack on the attention-seeking celebrities who enjoy the exhibitionism of their personal 'hardship'. George, who has always vowed to keep his private life sequestered cannot resist a bitchy dig at the fame game, 'Who gives a f**k about your problems darling?' As biographer Mick Middles so succinctly summed up; 'George's natural revulsion when faced with sycophants seeped into his song writing... a curious song to come from a talent so delicately poised on the verge of pretentiousness.' Indeed it is a little rich to hear such cattiness coming from an iconoclast so fickle himself. George has changed from thrusting himself into the spotlight as a sexy superstar during *Faith*, through his blanket refusal to promote *Listen Without Prejudice*, to his extensive interviews explaining his life-changing experiences as highlighted in *Older*.

You Have Been Loved
(George Michael / David Austin)

Following directly on from 'Jesus To A Child', 'You Have Been Loved' stems from Anselmo's death as George and Anselmo's mother, Alice, meet at the graveside to grieve openly together arm in arm. George described this tragic reversal in circumstance where a parent outlives her child as 'the ultimate pain because it is not supposed to happen that way... the ultimate test of faith almost inconceivable to me.' Standing out as one of the album's few unforeseen gems, this sincere and tender work deflects the attention away from George's customary first person narrative to the deathbed words of the dear departed. It was hardly surprising that the touching 'You Have Been Loved' was chosen to appear on the official commemorative album to mark the passing of Diana, Princess of Wales. For once George uses his vocal restraint to emphasise his probity, rather than detract from any emotion within the song, and the pathos comes across as genuine. Strange then that David Austin should resurface to co-write such an acutely personal piece.

Free
(George Michael)

George's first ever instrumental is a short-lived reprise of the mock Japanese Koto melody from 'The Strangest Thing', with brief bursts of ambient techno keyboards and the ever-present sampled string pad high in the bass-heavy mix. Notably George's third song to contain the word 'free' in the title, during the process of writing the album George has come full circle, and here exorcises his anguish and regret in favour of optimism for the future. How ironic that he is now 'free' (from his prohibitive recording contract with Sony) but can only bring himself to whisper it!

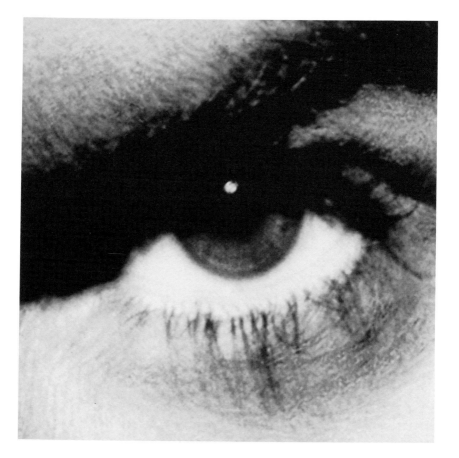

OLDER & UPPER

(AEGEAN / VIRGIN CDV 2802, RELEASED DECEMBER 1997)

It seemed that *Older* would never die as various singles from the original album were continually updated and released under the new guise of 'Radio Version' or alternative mixes. From the birth of 'Jesus To A Child' late in 1994 to the reincarnation of *Older & Upper* at the close of 1997, George incredibly managed to keep the same selection of songs alive and in the charts for an extended period of three years. Using the lure of an EP containing six new(ish) tracks and an interactive element, George revived *Older* as a stylish collectors' box set in an undemanding attempt to satisfy his fans' continual craving for a new product.

In essence the original *Older* has not changed, but has merely been placed with the six track bonus CD and presented in a box, with a close-up of George's eye adorning the cover. The more positively named *Upper* only merits a flimsy cardboard sleeve with an identical photograph – it will be of interest to hardcore hoarders to know that both CDs are gold in colour, ensuring that every George devotee can boast his or her very own gold disc! The truth of the matter is that all six tracks appearing on *Upper* had been previously released as extra tracks on the EPs promoting singles from *Older*. Additionally, a PC CD-ROM is required to play the interactive videos, and access to the Net is necessary to get the full benefit of the Website. Among others, *Q* magazine remarked in January 1998 how cheeky the re-release was, using the heading 'Old rope?' and suggesting that although the second release was safely distanced from the hype and expectations preceding *Older*, the public would undoubtedly resent forking out for what is essentially a repeat performance. Quibbles aside, *Older & Upper* is actually quite a nice collection to have as the majority of the music is excellent, the videos are stylish and enjoyable (if minuscule), and the sample Webpage is promising. George appears to be back on track in an encouragingly rejuvenated form as he cracked in *The Mirror* in 1997: 'I am not a miserable git. I am tired of transmitting pain.'

The inclusion of the interactive element stems from the fact that George's company Aegean is currently the most technically advanced record company on the Internet, with a staggering three million plus visitors in the first three months following its grand opening. George is a well-known cyberfreak and in 1997 became the first ever pop artist to limit his fan club, 'Members Online', exclusively to Net membership. Aegean rapidly set the revolutionary standard for other record labels by being the first company to allow their music to be downloaded online and create an A&R facility on the Site. The multi-media section on *Upper*, featuring three enhanced videos and a showcase of the Aegean Website, was made by a company called Abbey Road Interactive using Macromedia Director.

However futuristic this package may appear, George was yet again suffering from disagreements with the men in suits – this time with the North American DreamWorks team – and consequently *Older & Upper* has not been released in North America to date. George issued an embarrassed statement on the Aegean Website http://www.aegean.net , expressing his regret: 'most importantly I would like to apologise to many of my fans, especially those in the USA, for the lack of availability of my work in your country... my time so far with DreamWorks has been a frustrating and disappointing one.'

Fastlove Part II
(George Michael)

'Fastlove' sparkles on *Older* as a fresh and exciting dance track, yet pales in comparison next to its raunchier relation, 'Fastlove Part II'. Based more strongly around new vocals and Jo Bryant's breathy rendition of the 'Forget Me Nots' refrain, this punchy R&B mix demonstrates George's ability, when his heart is fully in it, to produce a brilliant, universally accessible dance track. George has removed the intrinsic flutey motif and the main verses of the original, instead favouring the strong

vocals, which are punctuated with a thumping bass and funky keyboard twiddles. Blasting out with an arresting beat, George selects the strongest section of the song and jumps straight in with the bridge. He also adds a catchy new chorus; 'Yeah yeah yeah / I got me some' and electronically doctored vocals which appear throughout *Upper*; 'gotta get up to get down'. 'Fastlove Part II' abruptly transforms into the rap sample and fuzzy bass line of 'I'm Your Man '96' as heard on *If You Were There – The Best of Wham!*, whose UK release was literally ten days before that of *Older & Upper*.

Spinning The Wheel
(Forthright Mix)
(George Michael / Jon Douglas)

Recalling Baby D's massive summer hit from 1995, '(Everybody's Got To Learn Sometime) I Need Your Loving', here George's floaty vocals are juxtaposed with an insistent drum 'n' bass backing. This clubby mix is courtesy of Forthright, a hip group of producers and personal friends of George, who specialise in remixes. The swing of 'Spinning The Wheel' has been replaced by a pounding, Hi-NRG beat which relies on a surprising amount of vocals for this genre, and although the mix is repetitive it is interesting to hear George placed against something quite so different. Designed as a chill-out breather, the high point of this track is the culmination of the sampled vocal snippets, effectively ending with the promise, 'I swear'.

Star People '97
(Radio Version)
(George Michael)

George laid down the vocals for 'Star People '97' just a couple of days after the death of his mother, commenting that 'it was almost like my way of putting my energy into something positive.' Indeed little of George's work has been more positive as he bitchily reasserts himself, and unlike the original really lets himself go, dropping all his recent vocal inhibitions. The lyrics are also spiced up with fresh barbs; 'Where the hell's my dumb ass PR' and 'Why do you wanna tell me that? / Get yourself some Oprah cash'. The music is fuller, incorporating extensive sampling from an old favourite of George and Andrew Ridgeley's, 'Burn Rubber On Me (Why You Wanna Hurt Me)' by The Gap Band, and emphasises the incessant dance rhythm with a bouncy bass, funky clavichord and radiant guitar. Andrew hits the brakes and screeches to a halt as first heard in the twelve inch version of 'I'm Your Man' from *Music From The Edge Of Heaven*, assisting the multi-layered vocal loop to soar to a dramatic climax at the end.

The Strangest Thing '97 (Radio Version)
(George Michael)

The Turkish terror returns replete with a twinkly but standard club beat which is hardly inspiring. George's pallid vocals have not been changed except to be bolstered by a higher octave. There is nothing special about this very basic rave mix and the unfortunate line 'I cannot seem to get my eyes open' has rarely been more applicable. The 'Take my life' closing refrain

regrettably translates as a possible suicide wish when taken out of context as it is here!

You Know That I Want To
(George Michael / Jon Douglas)

Q magazine described this snazzy trip-hop ballad as a 'spacey, midtempo tale of frustration' and certainly with 'You Know That I Want To' George perfectly approximates the laid-back feel of a drowsy Sunday morning. Recapitulating his former trademark accessible pop style yet updating it into a swing / soul context, George brings in a trippy keyboard line, smoochy bass and hints of muted trumpet to a quirky effect which accentuates the dance feel of the track. George sounds great as he shows off his effortless falsetto, and his writing, arranging and producing partnership with Jon Douglas hints towards a promising future. Warp speed ahead and welcome back!

Safe

(George Michael)

'Safe' is a spartan and edgy song of vulnerability that gets under your skin as it gradually builds up on its devastatingly effective loop. With disturbing lines like 'Someday my darkest fears will find their way' and 'It's hard not to feel this way / When you thought your future was on pre-scription', the words make you wonder whether this is perhaps an insight into George's state of mind after finishing with the drugs that saw him through the *Older* period. Lyrics aside, the ominous heart-beat and the anxious fluttering of the melody combine to produce a dark undercurrent, perfectly complimented by George's delicate and mournful voice. This beautifully crafted work comes to a close with an extended instrumental, using gorgeous guitar harmonics to heighten its heart-stopping effect.

INTERACTIVE ELEMENTS

On the 10th February 1997 George appeared at the Milia New Media Conference in Cannes to promote the launch of Aegean's Website. During the demonstration, George admitted that Aegean's technology had not yet been perfected and quipped; 'hopefully my lips will move in time to the music next time!' Along with the musical content, *Older & Upper* showcases a mini sample of the Aegean Website and three of George's promo videos from *Older*. The Website opens with a personal greeting from George's cousin Andreas Georgiou, who is also the President of Aegean. Although tantalising, there is actually little you can do without logging on to the Internet except study Wham! and George's discography which ironically omits the host package *Older & Upper*!

The three videos are entertaining and inventive, although the image is hardly bigger than a matchbox and is somewhat overshadowed by a looming picture of the familiar shadowed portrait from *Older*. As the videos date back a couple of years the underlying theme is one of insecurity, despair and sexual ambiguity as explored on *Older*, while bizarre exotic creatures wearing horned head-dresses dance their way throughout the clips.

Fastlove

Directed by Vaughan & Anthea, the trendy team famous for their striking adverts promoting Kiss FM and Levi's Jeans, the video for 'Fastlove' interprets the casual sex of the lyrics with stylish shape-shifting supermodels manipulated by George's knuckle-duster remote control. George's well known passion for hi-fis has perhaps gone too far as throughout these erotic displays of alternative pleasure he surveys the scene from a futuristic speaker throne. There is also a naughty dig at Sony as one of the dancers sports large headphones displaying the fake brand name 'Fony'. George finally consents to joining his subjects in dancing under a barrage of rain, soon to become the source of many sought-after photographic out-takes. Unfortunately, this must have been the video to which George referred when he commented that the words were out of synch with the film, thus sadly belying its professionalism.

Jesus To A Child

This was the first sight of George's new image with his smart suit, trimmed goatee and Caesar-style haircut. 'Jesus' symbolically deals with its harrowing mortality using swinging pendulums, broken sandcastles and a naked character lying in the foetal position. George's furrowed brow is prominent in this artistic visual interpretation of genuine pain.

Spinning The Wheel

As with 'Fastlove', the video for 'Spinning The Wheel' literally depicts the lyrics; in this case the idea of dicing with death is portrayed by a gun being loaded for a fatal game of Russian roulette. The monochrome setting is a Twenties jazz club full of gangsters, flappers and girlie singers covertly revelling in the years of prohibition. George is the jazz singer in impenetrable shades with Latin dancers gyrating on the floor in front of him. In a flash back to the video for 'I Want Your Sex' where George lipsticks the words 'Explore Monogamy' on Kathy Jeung's body, 'Spinning The Wheel' potently shows a woman with the oxymoron of 'Trust' and 'Lust' on her naked back.

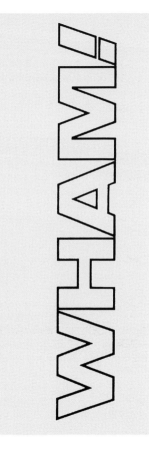

COMPILATION ALBUMS
THE FINAL

(EPIC EPC 88681, RELEASED JULY 1986)

Released as an alternative to the American *Music From The Edge Of Heaven*, *The Final* co-ordinated with Wham!'s farewell concert in both title and packaging. The inner sleeve shows the changing looks, clothing, hair and stubble length of our boys during the period 1982-1986. George claims he was not consciously aiming to make a statement in adorning a new image for each album but merely going through a natural style progression: 'I was still a kid trying to work out which way I looked best.'

The tracks are a mixture of Wham!'s first two albums, the highlights of the *Music From The Edge Of Heaven* album and three new mixes. The original vinyl pressing also featured the track 'Blue (Armed With Love)', but this was dropped for the CD release.

Track Listing:

Wham! Rap (Enjoy What You Do?) / Young Guns (Go For It!) / Bad Boys / Club Tropicana / Wake Me Up Before You Go-Go / Careless Whisper / Freedom / Last Christmas (Pudding Mix) / Everything She Wants (Remix) / I'm Your Man / A Different Corner / Battlestations / Where Did Your Heart Go? / The Edge Of Heaven

Careless Whisper
(George Michael / Andrew Ridgeley)

This version of 'Careless Whisper' is the popular single release which loses the lengthy synthesised introduction and stark first verse as featured on

Wham!'s second album, *Make It Big*. Launching straight into that famous sax melody, this one gets straight to the point and pulls no poignant punches.

Everything She Wants (Remix)
(George Michael)

Updated for *The Final*, this track is a minute and a half longer than the original on *Make It Big*, adding a new bridge and suitable lyrics: 'My situation never changes / Walking in and out of that door / Like a stranger, but one with the wages / I give you all that you say you want and more'. George's voice has noticeably matured as he sings the altered second half with more gusto, and he has also padded out the rest of the song accordingly with a longer introduction, using sustained chords and various new keyboard stabs.

I'm Your Man
(George Michael)

The seven inch single release of 'I'm Your Man' was dismissed as lightweight by the disdainful critics, but unsurprisingly reached the top of the charts nonetheless. This version is missing the extended animated introduction that appears on *Music From The Edge Of Heaven*, but certainly does not suffer from its loss! As with *The Final*'s adaptation of 'Careless Whisper', this shortened track bounds straight in with its infectious four-on-the-floor beat, but sadly does not include Deon Estus' effervescent bass solo.

TWELVE INCH MIXES —
WHAM!

(EPIC EPC 450125 2, RELEASED NOVEMBER 1992)

Wham! Rap
(Enjoy What You Do?)
(Unsocial Mix)
(George Michael / Andrew Ridgeley)

This hard-hitting mix uses the updated vocal performance from *Music From The Edge Of Heaven*'s 'Wham! Rap '86', but thankfully omits the irritating samples and is musically closer to the original Bob Carter version. The combination works very well as a straightforward twelve inch and is a fun, lively opener to this collection.

Young Guns (Go For It!)
(George Michael)

Boosting the vocals and strengthening the disco atmosphere with excitable whooping and yelling, this twelve inch mix is even more confident than the original and sees Wham! rocking with their collars turned firmly up.

Freedom (Long Mix)
(George Michael)

An intriguingly different beginning of vocals and organ leads into a standard instrumental version of the entire first verse and chorus of 'Freedom' before finally starting the song. This 'Long Mix' is aptly titled and instantly loses all impact, stunting an essentially perfect snappy pop song.

Everything She Wants
(Remix)
(George Michael)

This is the same version as the track reviewed on *The Final*.

I'm Your Man
(Extended Stimulation)
(George Michael)

The 'Extended Stimulation' mix, also known as the 'Magic Car' remix, begins with a triumphant 'I'm Your Man' and initially continues as per the track found on *Music From The Edge Of Heaven*, car crash and all. At some point however, someone felt it would be appropriate to introduce a conversation between a conniving George, his latest conquest and unnervingly, George's gearstick, in the voice of Mike Oldfield's renowned Piltdown Man; 'Oh come on, I just wanna be your big boy...! Thankfully Deon's more stimulating bass solo soon brings us back down to earth!

Various other incarnations of *Twelve Inch Mixes* have been available in different formats, but have since been deleted. A George Michael fan with a keen eye would do well to pick up the most comprehensive of these cancelled official releases, *The Twelve Inch Tape* (Epic

450125 4, Released December 1992), which has the following track listing:

Wham! Rap / Careless Whisper / Freedom / Everything She Wants / I'm Your Man (Extended Stimulation) / Wham! Rap (Club Mix) / Careless Whisper (Instrumental Version) / Freedom / Everything She Wants / I'm Your Man

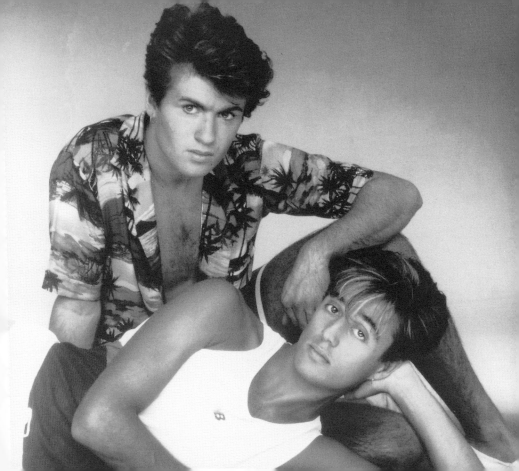

THE BEST OF
WHAM!

THE BEST OF WHAM! –
IF YOU WERE THERE

(EPIC EPC 489020 2, RELEASED NOVEMBER 1997)

Contractual obligations are the name of the game here, with George agreeing to release this 'Best Of' compilation to satisfy Sony with two additional new songs. Launched in tandem with the corresponding video at the end of 1997, this was purely a Christmas package aimed to entice a younger generation of listeners. At the time of writing, a further solo 'Greatest Hits' double compilation album is planned to fill 1998's festive stockings.

George's involvement in the project included designing the sleeve (which is virtually unreadable in tiny silver text) and the two new offerings. It is a shame that the original recordings were not digitally remastered but thankfully, as this is a 'Best Of' rather than a 'Greatest Hits' album, George's personally attributed nadir, 'Bad Boys', is absent from the track listing. *Record Collector* quite rightly noted in their review that *The Best of Wham! – If You Were There* is 'a bit of a rip-off – ten of the fifteen tracks can still be found on their still-available hits collection, *The Final*.' For newcomers to Wham! however this is probably the best introduction to one of the greatest Eighties bands on the market.

Track Listing:

If You Were There / I'm Your Man / Everything She Wants / Club Tropicana / Wake Me Up Before You Go-Go / Like A Baby / Freedom / The Edge Of Heaven / Wham! Rap / Young Guns (Go For It!) / Last Christmas / Where Did Your Heart Go? / Everything She Wants '97 / I'm Your Man '96

Everything She Wants '97
(George Michael)

George has often mentioned that 'Everything She Wants' is one of his favourite self-penned songs, so it comes as no surprise that here it is again in an updated, uptempo dance incarnation. Fulfilling the remainder of his contract with Sony, George produced this disco flavoured floor-filler with layered female backing vocals, brass stabs, guitars and a pumping club beat added to most of the original keyboard parts. He also laid down a new, relaxed lead vocal which emphasises that his singing ability didn't really disappear with the recording of *Older* the previous year.

I'm Your Man '96
(George Michael)

This '96 version sees George emerging from the lethargy of *Older*. As with 'Everything She Wants '97', it is co-produced by George and Jon Douglas, and the latter provides the link to the single released by Lisa Moorish as reviewed in the Miscellaneous section of this book. The busy party atmosphere of the track is almost identical to that of George's duet with Lisa, whose only uncredited appearance here is the 'One, Two, Three, Four' line which is peppered throughout. George has added an impressive new vocal and proves that he can swing with the best of them!

CLUB FANTASTIC MEGAMIX

(RELEASED NOVEMBER 1983)

The *Club Fantastic Megamix* was rush released by Mark Dean of Innervision during the period that the label was seeking an injunction against Wham!, prohibiting them from signing with another record company. Choosing three of the four non-singles from the boys' well-milked début album, *Fantastic*, Dean released the twelve inch disc late in 1983 and due to the unfulfilled demand for Wham! products it soon reached Number 15 in the UK charts in November. This success was despite George's adamant disapproval, as expressed in Wham!'s scathing press release: 'It's absolutely disgusting. I just hope the radio doesn't play it. It would be so irritating to hear something you think is so bad.'

The three tracks lifted from the album were 'A Ray Of Sunshine', 'Come On!' and The Miracles' cover, 'Love Machine', played respectively and then reversed.

The flipside is a similar instrumental concoction. The mix itself is not quite as bad as the young George would have led us to believe and is actually a fairly respectable slice of boogie. The only aspects that are truly wince-worthy are the imposed perpetual echoes producing an annoying vocal loop and the clumsy segueing of the tracks, especially around 'Love Machine' with its incompatible tempo. *Record Mirror* reviewed that the cobbled together cash-in 'should be retitled 'Club Fantastic Cement Mix'.' Although the duo never benefited financially from this release, *Club Fantastic Megamix*'s overt Seventies influence and insistent beat ensured that any 'Wham! To Split' rumours were deflected at the time and kept the group in the public eye until their private legal battles were resolved.

MISCELLANEOUS

George Michael has proved to be a source of delight to collectors of rarities and anomalous tracks. After the heady and commercial days of Wham! when it was more the picture than the product that counted, George recognised that in his solo career he could sell more records by tapping into the B-side market, and promptly endeavoured to establish himself as a 'collectable' artist. This desire can be seen in the transcript of the court case against Sony in 1993, where George explains that 'B-sides are normally seen as some kind of second rate piece of material, but certain other artists that I have noticed in the last four of five years have been really making a feature of new material for B-sides... there's an incentive for them to buy the single, even though they already have the album.' Considering that George has not been particularly prolific in releasing new albums, the following 26 miscellaneous tracks form a welcome addition to his back catalogue.

GUESTING ON OTHER ARTISTS' TRACKS

George has always been eager to quietly contribute to the music of his friends and influential childhood idols, gladly lending his chart-friendly backing vocals or accomplished production skills. His modesty occasionally leads to ambiguity, as was the case with the 1987 Boogie Box High release, 'Jive Talkin'', a project put together by his cousin Andreas Georgiou. The speculation that had George singing and Nick Heyward playing guitar no doubt assisted the ascent of the archetypal Eighties rejuvenation of the Bee Gees' disco classic to its Number 7 placement in the UK. Another unassuming appearance was on David Cassidy's Top 10 comeback single 'Last Kiss', three years earlier in November 1984. This unusual and somewhat generous collaboration was largely due to the fact that George had grown up watching the youthful heart-throb on the kids' programme *Saturday Scene*, and that the two artists happened to share the same publisher. More recently George has been heard contributing vocals to Aegean's latest prodigy, Trigger, on the song 'Chameleon (Shed Your Skin)'.

Heaven Help Me – Deon Estus

(Deon Estus / George Michael)

George's long-time bassist Deon Estus commenced his solo career as a support artist for George on his *Faith* tour. Within the tight schedule George aided Deon extensively on his début album *Spell*; co-writing, producing and singing backing vocals on 'Heaven Help Me' in particular. All the usual Wham! crew were present including Hugh Burns (guitar), Danny Schogger (keyboards), Paul Spong and Steve Sidwell (horns). This mild mannered pop song spent six weeks in the US Top 20 peaking at Number 4 in April 1989, but did not fair quite so well in the UK where it just skimmed the Top 40. Strikingly similar to the Human League's 'Human' (a Top 10 hit on both sides of Atlantic in 1986) the music is hesitant and gentle, showing Deon's voice to be remarkably similar to George's, although he perhaps lacks the confidence to fully 'let go' as George would on 'Father Figure'. The two voices blend well together in the chorus as they sing a familiar tale of heartbreak and broken dreams.

Nikita – Elton John
(Elton John / Bernie Taupin)

Having been friends with Seventies rock superstar Elton John since the days of *Make It Big*, George was delighted when his former role model asked him to provide vocal support for the seasoned star's comeback album, *Ice On Fire*. George shared backing vocals with Elton and Davey Johnstone, and the overall Eighties appeal was heightened with the appearance of singer / songwriter Nik Kershaw on guitar. 'Nikita' is an easy-going tale of love divided by distance, whose bland and slow-paced melody reaches a synthetic climax, featuring George's sweet falsetto which

glides over the closing chorus. This song was released as the first single from *Ice On Fire* and rested a couple of places behind 'I'm Your Man' in the Top 10 in late 1985.

Wrap Her Up – Elton John featuring George Michael
(Elton John / Bernie Taupin)

The second single from *Ice On Fire*, 'Wrap Her Up', included several veteran musicians from the days of Wham! as well as George; Charlie Morgan, Paul Spong, Raul D'Oliveira and Rick Taylor among others. The backing vocals also included Kiki Dee, who joined Andrew Ridgeley on Elton and George's performance of 'Don't Let The Sun Go Down On Me' at Live Aid that same year. 'Wrap Her Up' is a high-spirited rocky tribute to women the world over, with George lending particular falsetto assistance throughout the verses. This jaunty track culminates in a frenetic free-for-all where the singers nominate their favourite females: Samantha Fox, Grace Jones, Joan Collins, Nancy

Reagan and Shirley Temple to name but a few – even George's frequent companion 'Miss Pat Fernandez' gets a mention! Considerably involved in this project, George also made a brief appearance in the accompanying video, and this venture merely pinpointed the restriction that Wham! as a group was imposing on George as an artist. As 1985 changed to 1986 the increasingly successful George could be heard on no less than four singles in the Top 20 with 'Wrap Her Up', re-releases of 'Last Christmas' and 'Do They Know It's Christmas?', and the current Wham! anthem 'I'm Your Man'.

DUETS

Desafinado – Astrud Gilberto and George Michael

(Antonio Carlos Jobim / Newton Mendonca)

Written by the man who inspired the Brazilian flavour of the album *Older*, Antonio Carlos Jobim, this bossa nova classic was originally an instrumental hit in 1962 for guitarist Charlie Byrd and saxophonist Stan Getz. George performs this duet version of the song thirty years later with high-pitched songstress Astrud Gilberto, who had achieved early fame in the Sixties with such hits as 'The Girl From Ipanema', another Jobim standard. If you like bossa nova then this is the song for you, although the average George fan might find it a little hard to stomach! Against an airy, light backing with twinkling piano and sleepy sax, the pairing of the two voices is perhaps unwise as they tend to stray off key when singing in unison. Astrud's girlish tones come across as

inexpressive and dull while George is no doubt intimidated by the prospect of singing in Portuguese. 'Desafinado' can be found on the 'Older' EP and also the ninth AIDS charity produced *Red Hot + Rio* album, a collection by artists such as PM Dawn, Sting and David Byrne covering the songs of the late Antonio Carlos Jobim. At the time of writing, George had publicly earmarked 'Desafinado' to appear on his forthcoming 'Greatest Hits' compilation album.

Don't Let The Sun Go Down On Me – George Michael / Elton John

(Elton John / Bernie Taupin)

This revamped version of the Elton John hit from 1974 was first performed by a reverent George at Live Aid in 1985, with Elton accompanying him on piano. The song was released on EP years later, having been recorded live as an emotional duet in London in March

1991, and can also be found on Elton John's *Duets* album. 'Don't Let The Sun Go Down On Me' was a Number 1 in sixteen countries in the year the Sony trial commenced, becoming George's tenth US chart topper the following February. Typical of the generosity from artists of their magnitude and era, the proceeds were distributed to various children's, AIDS and cancer charities based in the UK and the US. Opening with a dynamic 'Imagine'-style piano solo, George hurls himself into a torrid rendition of this enduring ballad, having found the confidence to suffuse his vocals with a passion that unfortunately borders on luvvie-esque falsity. The mutual appreciation society of George and Elton with their overblown chumminess can be a little hard to swallow at times, even though we all know it's for a good cause.

I Knew You Were Waiting (For Me) – Aretha Franklin and George Michael
(Dennis Morgan / Simon Climie)

This powerful duet succeeded in its objectives of presenting George as a credible solo artist and reasserting the Sixties soul diva Aretha Franklin as a viable commercial product. Instigated by Aretha, the pairing was quite literally conceived in a boardroom purely for mutual gain, bringing George in as the 'acceptable honky'. George travelled to Detroit to record the rock / soul crossover with Aretha during the wind-up of Wham! and the resulting single was released in 1987, sensationally bridging the gap between *The Final* and *Faith*. 'I Knew You Were Waiting' ironically kept former Wham!-ettes Pepsi and Shirlie at Number 2 with their début single, 'Heartache'.

The winning collaboration of George and Aretha was complemented by emerging at a time of chart soul revival and predictably continued George's

string of hits while providing Aretha with her first Number 1 in nearly twenty years (consequently appearing on her *Aretha* album). The phenomenal hit demonstrated late Eighties pop at its best in skilfully fusing elements of white pop and black R&B. George was astute enough to realise that it would be futile to compete with the vocal acrobatics of the seasoned singer and instead simply maintained the melody while Aretha ad-libbed. Winning the 1987 Grammy award for Best R&B Vocal Performance was second nature to Aretha who had claimed the title ten times previously, but it was a tremendous honour for George, who enthused that it 'validates the tremendous influence R&B music has had on my music, songwriting and creative process. Not bad a for Brit with Soul.' The union came to an uneasy conclusion the following year upon George's release of his next single, 'I Want Your Sex', when Aretha publicly condemned his lyrics by stating they were 'too dirty' in the press.

I'm Your Man – Lisa Moorish
(George Michael)

Self-confessed George Michael fanatic Lisa Moorish put forward the successful idea of releasing a cover version of Wham!'s 'I'm Your Man' to producer Jon Douglas. Having previously worked with top Brit soulsters Gabrielle and Eternal, as a result of this project Douglas went on to work with George on future material, including several tracks on the *Older* album. Initially dubious, the high-flying producer remembers, 'We started to work on it and a Tape Op at Sarm got a copy to George. He strolled in and was really supportive, even adding some uncredited backing vocals.' George in fact sings the second verse and really lets loose on this sexy, gender-bending adaptation incorporating a cheesy rap by The Scientists Of Sound. The vampish Lisa, known for her Eighties-style club music, dominates the duet sounding like a modern day Eartha Kitt.

Learn To Say No – Jody Watley featuring George Michael

(George Michael / Richard Fields)

This surprisingly rock-orientated duet developed as a result of George's participation in the Band Aid project in late 1984, where he met established dance artiste, Jody Watley. Jody had tentatively started her career in the late Seventies as a teenager dancing on the music programme Soul Train, and made her breakthrough as a vocalist with the American disco group Shalamar. Having enjoyed mainstream success during the early Eighties, she went on to a Grammy Award winning solo career. 'Learn To Say No' occurred as both Jody and George Michael were launching their individual début albums, and its unrelenting Robert Palmer beat allows the pair to strut their stuff and become rock stars for the day. The lavish sound of the heavy slap bass hook and electric power drums is entertaining but is really just a simple stomping standard – it is

however George's full-on Faith-era vocals, spikily complimented by Jody's unexpected rock input that makes the song. 'Learn To Say No' can be found on Jody's eponymous album, Jody Watley.

Waltz Away Dreaming – Toby Bourke

(George Michael / Toby Bourke)

Toby Bourke was the first artist to be signed to George's fledgling label Aegean and this duet was the company's first release accordingly. George had heard Toby's enchanting demo just a couple of nights after the loss of his mother Lesley to cancer, and adapted the lyrics into a touching tribute in the hope that it would help his father come to terms with the passing of his wife. Toby assumes the role of George's father in the duet, which explores both aspects of the family bereavement; 'She'll come to you in disguise / She's there in your children's eyes / Still our mother / She's still your wife'. The music is purposely kept simple with just

a bass, acoustic guitar and piano, enveloped by Enya-esque backing vocals. 'Waltz Away Dreaming' was donated to the Help A London Child charity in order to raise funds for London's less advantaged children. Capital Radio listeners were asked to pledge money to hear an exclusive first play of the single on Easter Sunday 1997 and George vowed to give £2 for every £1 raised, but added 'If Elton John or Richard Branson ring, tell them I was only joking!' A staggering total of £1 million was raised for the cause and in a speech at the Capital Radio charity lunch George declared, 'My mother was a woman of great compassion, she was proud to be associated with what I do for Help A London Child.'

RED HOT + DANCE

Red Hot + Dance was the second major album produced by the Red Hot Organisation, a charity dedicated to raising money and awareness for AIDS. High calibre artists such as Madonna, Seal and Lisa Stansfield donated their tracks for remixing courtesy of hip mixers Sly and Robbie, Frankie Knuckles and Nellee Hooper to name but a few. George instead chose to contribute three previously unreleased songs to the worthy cause, tracks which had originally been intended to appear on the dance-orientated 'Listen Without Prejudice Volume II'. During the Sony trial George explained to the Chancery High Court, 'It was actually a remix album... I was going to give them a track from *Listen Without Prejudice* to remix and then... when I decided that I was not going to make a dance album, or even half a dance album, I decided almost immediately after that to give those three tracks.' The organisation was understandably flattered by George's generosity and praised his unpublicised help on the album's sleeve notes; 'his work behind the scenes ensured that this LP saw the light of day.' George's tracks certainly grab the attention as the rest of *Red Hot + Dance* is remarkably understated for an album of its genre, consisting mostly of fairly standard remixes of the featured artists' early Nineties chart smashes.

Too Funky
(George Michael)

The opening track on *Red Hot + Dance* begins with a startlingly clipped Hollywood accent, 'I am not trying to seduce you' before launching into this immaculate dance track with the tantalising proposition, 'Would you like me to seduce you / Is that what you're trying to tell me?' Seemingly influenced by Jocelyn Brown's 1984 enduring club standard, 'Somebody Else's Guy', the sample heaven of 'Too Funky' is a polished accumulation of Eighties and contemporary early Nineties dance favourites. The disjointed intro, peppered with snatches of vocals from songs past and present, confidently builds up with the introduction of a clubby bass and bright housey piano, before the entry of George's familiar anti-chastity tease, 'Hey, you're just too funky for me / I gotta get inside of you'. George alternates between breathy frustration and macho insinuation in this accomplished dance track which finishes as abruptly as it starts – with an exhausted, fed-up cry for George to stop playing with his radio, thus belying the musical fragmentation. The public lapped up this sure-fire dance hit, guaranteeing the single a respectable place in the UK Top 5.

Do You Really Want To Know
(George Michael)

Bouncing straight into the second song on *Red Hot + Dance*, this monotonous piece of Europop sadly drops to the lowest level of the compilation rather than continuing the inspired flair of 'Too Funky'. The driving rhythm, light, breezy trumpet and vocal non-entity fail to ignite and the song is remarkably similar to the Stock Aitken & Waterman production line of the mid to late Eighties. Although lyrically George tries to redeem his lustful implications of 'Too Funky' with a message of safe sex; 'The world is full of lovers / Night after night, week after week / Trusting to look in the pocketful of rubbers', his wording retains a boy-band degree of clumsiness. With its simplistic teenybopper repetition, 'Do You Really Want To Know' comes as a disappointing let down in George's otherwise excellent dance repertoire.

Happy
(George Michael)

George reiterates his safe sex stance with his third and final contribution to *Red Hot + Dance:* a snappy house number complete with muted trumpet swirls and a catchy bass line. His low register, intimate vocals paint a vivid picture of a scheming bisexual prostitute's sordid solicitation. George cannot understand how anyone can sell themselves for sex, purely on a profit basis: 'Lay me down lay me down / For that big stash cheap cash think about the money'. He continues to denounce the hooker's morals with the self-righteous snipe; 'You don't dig men / But you'll f**k 'em if they're rich / You can't be with me / You're a low-life, daughterofasonofabitch'. Thus ends the trilogy of uptempo sex education.

UNPLUGGED

George performed his contribution for the popular MTV series, *Unplugged*, in the informal setting of the Three Mills Studios, London on 11th October 1996. Whilst the programme has been broadcast the world over several times and four of the songs have been released on the EPs promoting *Older*, the full recording and video have yet to be released as a package in their own right. The public demand for this show has resulted in the marketing of many bootlegs and has also sparked off rumours about the contractual obligations of both George and DreamWorks. As George signed to the American label for just two albums of which *Older* was the first, it is possible that a commercial release of *Unplugged* could constitute George's second album for DreamWorks, therefore ending his contract before time allowed a full remuneration of their initial investment. However, Aegean state on their Website FAQ section that the reason for non-release of the product is simply that, 'MTV hold the right to that footage and we cannot re-publish it ourselves.'

George is joined for his performance by many familiar faces; Hugh Burns, Chris Cameron and Andy Hamilton are among the band which also constitutes a string section – somewhat extravagant for an *Unplugged* line-up. Jo Bryant makes an appearance along with Shirley Lewis among the backing vocalists, and George for his part is in good voice, although his visual presentation is restricted as he doesn't move from his stool, centre stage. The arrangements of the songs are professional and slick, translating well into an intimate acoustic setting and it is a shame that the concert has not been released in its entirety with the promotion it deserves. The four approved out-takes have been reviewed below.

Everything She Wants
(George Michael)

Featuring on the 'Star People' EP,

'Everything She Wants' is the only song performed for *Unplugged* that dates back to the Wham! era, eloquently proving that a good song will always stand the test of time in the right hands. In 1996, 'Everything She Wants' was nearly thirteen years old and here it has been successfully revamped from the sterile Eighties electronic backing loop into a smooth, mature rendition, with acoustic guitars, organ and piano adding a new dimension. Even George's original automated harmonies have been updated into a stylish gospel chorus. His personal interjections are amusing with such comments as 'I'm doing all the work!' quipped in his best Hertfordshire accent.

Father Figure
(George Michael)

George's *Unplugged* performance of *Faith*'s 'Father Figure' appears on the 'You Have Been Loved' EP. The original's eastern flavoured string pad has been replaced by a twinkling bell tree and a real string section, while Shirley Lewis' straight gospel vocals are bolstered by a full, more syncopated chorus. This performance succeeds by exaggerating the highlights of the

original and amplifying the difference in size, impact and volume between the chorus and verses. An attractively gentle piano sequence supports George's rich voice which is powerfully emotive and faultless in its phrasing. He plays to the gallery with an overlong break at the end: 'I will be the one who loves you... till the end of... time'.

Praying For Time
(George Michael)

The substantial changes made on 'Everything She Wants' and 'Father Figure' have not been applied to 'Praying For Time', which remains a socially aware ballad. However, the overbearing string pad of the original has again been replaced by the real thing, with the addition of a piano lending an even greater resemblance to the work of John Lennon. With such a sparse backing, attention is focussed on George's slightly booming voice which is a tad too high in the mix for comfort. 'Praying For Time' in its *Unplugged* format is available on the 'You Have Been Loved' EP.

Star People
(George Michael)

Closing the 'Star People' EP, the *Unplugged* version of this bitchy dance number provides a traceable link between the original on *Older* and the remixed 'Star People '97' found on *Upper*. Whilst retaining the laid-back vocals of the first it then introduces a vibrancy and drive not heard on *Older* with a spiky guitar and percussion, and Jo Bryant's backing vocals replaced with the obligatory full chorus. Especially effective is the introduction which has acapella vocals punctuated by a solo bass drum before the band plunges into the main part of the song. This performance is clearly enjoyed by both George and the appreciative audience and was undoubtedly a highlight of the evening.

GENERAL
MISCELLANEOUS

Crazyman Dance
(George Michael)

Appearing as one of the various B-sides of 'Too Funky', 'Crazyman Dance' is a vitriolic attack on the treatment of New York's homeless immigrants living in poverty – territory previously explored by Phil Collins' Number 1 social comment 'Another Day In Paradise' in 1989. George felt strongly on the subject of the homeless, anonymously volunteering at Holborn's soup kitchen and openly criticising modern society in an interview with Chris Evans for Radio One in 1996: 'There shouldn't be people with their hands out on the street... no government is ever going to be able to do anything about this.'

Although George's ethic is to encourage self-help rather than charity, in this song he expresses the sheer desperation of the beggar on the street, forced to perform for the occasional meagre donation from an uncomfortable passer-by: 'Why don't you look at my face / Why don't you look in my eyes / You'd rather look at your feet / You'd rather look at the skies'. In a gravelly voice infused with spite and hatred, George sings of the overwhelming oppression of the big city: 'Yesterday's newspapers / I wrap them around my body / Outside these skyscrapers', with the echo of his voice reverberating in a desperate plea. The brutal metropolitan aspect is reflected in the music with an immense, cluttered loop incorporating sirens, wailing babies and street sounds. The reality of the failed American dream is a big brother to the conscientious message of the track 'Hand To Mouth' from *Faith*.

Fantasy
(George Michael)

'Fantasy' appeared as a B-side to 'Freedom 90', on the 'Waiting For That Day' EP and also on a free, four-track cassette generously issued by George at his *Cover To Cover* shows at Wembley. Built on a repetitive bass riff interspersed with bursts of brass, 'Fantasy' bears a certain resemblance to Deee-Lite's transatlantic 1990 Top 5 hit, 'Groove Is In The Heart'. A quirkier track than George normally produces, 'Fantasy' is jolly enough with its squealing trumpet, easy-going lyrics and persistent dance rhythm.

Freedom
(Back To Reality Mix)
(George Michael / B Romeo / C Wheeler / N Hooper / S Law)

In the same manner that George cunningly spliced 'Killer' with 'Papa Was A Rollin' Stone' on the *Five Live* EP, here he fuses his personal emancipation plea, 'Freedom 90', with Soul II Soul's 1989 world-wide smash, 'Back To Life (However Do You Want Me)' which George had previously performed on his *Cover To Cover* tour. With a similar fluency the bass line is used as a

linking feature between the two songs, and although George uses samples of the drum track from 'Back To Life', he replaces Caron Wheeler's summery vocals with his own and fluidly combines them with excerpts from 'Freedom 90'. The mix is energetic and bright with the inclusion of 'Back To Life''s jaunty Irish jig, and stands out as the only non-live track on the 'Don't Let The Sun Go Down On Me' EP released in 1991. 'Freedom (Back To Reality Mix)' can also be found on the Wembley four track cassette.

I Believe (When I Fall In Love It Will Be Forever)
(S Wonder / Y Wright)

This live song was the B-Side to 'Don't Let The Sun Go Down On Me', on the EP of the same name and also on the Wembley four track cassette. Stevie Wonder's religious lyrics are an atypical choice for George as he has never before expressed any kind of religious leaning in his work; 'God's soul answered my prayers / Won't you listen to me now'. 'I Believe' is a song in two parts commencing with a romantic ballad in a traditional format with the emphasis placed heavily on the chorus. It then progresses to the funkier second half with a rising bass line and a stirring sax. The audience clearly enjoys the transition, yet when George attempts his notorious sing-a-long section the lacklustre response is pretty painful.

I Can't Make You Love Me
(Reid / Shamblin)

'I Can't Make You Love Me' is a touching Bonnie Raitt song that has also been recently covered by The Artist Formerly Known As Prince and included on his *Emancipation* triple album. George's version can be found on the 'Older' EP and single, and although it has never been released as an A-side to date, George announced in his welcoming letter to Aegean's Website that 'I Can't Make You Love Me' will appear on his future 'Greatest Hits' project.

In adapting this beautiful love song to

suit his style, George has slightly relaxed the tempo of Bonnie's version, allowing more intimacy and sentiment to filter through in his exquisite performance. The orchestration is charmingly simplistic following a similar fashion to 'Waltz Away Dreaming' with just bass, acoustic guitar, piano and a muffled drum pattern. Occasionally the understated strings and graceful backing harmonies compliment the arrangement. George's voice has rarely been more moving; his pure falsetto is particularly heart-stopping. The song as a whole is incredibly well-paced, with a slow, powerful build-up that never strays from the restraint that forms the heart of the song. If the music is not enough, then listen to the lyrics describing a selfless lover accepting an impending break-up, with the eternal hope that 'someone's gonna love me'. The perfect ballad.

If You Were My Woman
(P Sawyer / C Macmurry / G Jones)

After George's rendition of Marvin Gaye's 'Sexual Healing' was so well received at the Nelson Mandela Freedom Concert at Wembley, he planned to release a Motown cover. He chose to adapt Gladys Knight's 1970 hit 'If I Were Your Woman' to reflect the gender change, and intended all proceeds to go to various anti-apartheid groups. Unfortunately this never materialised and the live recording of 'If You Were My Woman' can consequently be found on the 'Don't Let The Sun Go Down On Me' EP, the Wembley four track cassette and also as the B-side to 'Praying For Time'. The rather simplistic arrangement is fairly boring, with George coming across as a bland stadium crooner – the audience seems less than enthusiastic.

Love's In Need Of Love Today
(Stevie Wonder)

George first performed the 1976 Stevie Wonder composition, 'Love's In Need Of Love Today' with Stevie at the Motown fiftieth anniversary celebration at Harlem's Apollo Theatre in New York City in May, 1985. He later released a solo live recording as the B-side to 'Father Figure'. While Stevie's original is mellow, warm and unhurried, George's version doesn't really get off the ground as it somehow loses its gooey feel-good charm. Although he adds hi-hats for rhythmic interest and modernises the chorus, it is obvious that George has chosen the song for personal reasons, citing in *The South Bank Show* that he feels Stevie's vocal range matches his own perfectly. However his fans are probably too young to know the track and such an intimate song is a rather curious choice for the close of a live show.

The Strangest Thing (Live)
(George Michael)

It seemed the reign of the Turkish terror would never cease as George performed this live at the BBC Radio Theatre on 8th October 1996, in preparation for the *Unplugged* session. Appearing on the 'Older' EP, 'The Strangest Thing (Live)' is by far the best version of the three recordings available (as opposed to the original *Older* recording and the *Older & Upper* remix). Setting a relaxed pace with real instruments replacing their synthesised counterparts, George's vocal is more involved and he has improved the backing harmonies of the 'la la la' refrain.

Tonight
(Elton John / Bernie Taupin)

George's contribution to the tribute album *Two Rooms – Celebrating The Songs Of Elton John & Bernie Taupin*, was this odious live recording from Wembley Arena in March 1991. George had eagerly purchased Elton's album

Blue Moves on the day of its release and later gushed 'Even though I was only 13 years old, 'Tonight' was possibly the most moving song I had ever heard.' The vastly extended tinkling piano and synthesised orchestral introduction is a full two minutes and sixteen seconds too long. 'Tonight' fares no better with the commencement of George's melodramatic vocal, that is so similar to that of Elton John's, it sounds as though he has overdosed on his hero's recordings.

Too Jazzy (Happy Mix)
(George Michael)

Appearing as one of the B-sides to 'Too Funky', for 'Too Jazzy (Happy Mix)' the vocal melody of 'Too Funky' has simply been placed over the keyboard sequence and drum loop of 'Happy'. The result is a strangely downbeat oddity, which slowly transforms via the familiar muted trumpet swirl into the original sound of 'Happy'. A bit of an artistic cop-out, but harmless enough.

SON OF ALBERT
ANDREW RIDGELEY

(EPIC EPC 4667172, RELEASED AUGUST 1990)

Track Listing:

Red Dress / Shake / The Price Of Love / Flame / Hangin' / Mexico / Big Machine / Kiss Me / Baby
Jane / Shake (Hardcore)

Andrew Ridgeley's one and only solo offering was one of the worst received albums of 1990, achieving only half a star in a dreadful *Rolling Stone* review. It fared no better in the public eye, reaching a pitiful Number 130 in the US charts. Rather than the hard rock thrashings that have been suggested, the parentally eponymous *Son Of Albert* actually consists of mainstream, soft rock reiterations in the style of Def Leppard, but without the flair. Ridgeley's reedy and anonymous voice is disguised by being constantly multi-tracked, at times with other singers including George Michael in 'Red Dress'.

Lyrically limited, Ridgeley comes from the one verse / six choruses school of writing and the insistent, pounding guitars do not let up until the last song, 'Baby Jane'; a curious attempt at a blues number that needs a stronger voice to succeed. Largely co-written with Gary Brougham, *Son Of Albert* segues from one track to the next, with very little variety. A Queen influence can be briefly heard on 'Kiss Me', the cover

of The Everly Brothers' 'Price Of Love' is a non-stop nonentity and Ridgeley cannot seem to escape the spectre of Wham! with 'Mexico''s 'Whoo-hoo!'s and motorbike revving effects. The only mildly successful single, 'Shake', was co-written with Wham!'s mutual friend, David Austin, and also adapted into a 'hardcore' mix; a tuneless dirge of a bonus track for the CD release.

Andrew admitted recently to *Hello!*

magazine, 'It was disappointing and depressing to receive quite such a beating over that album. The whole thing had been tongue-in-cheek and it was misconstrued.' While the sales of *Son* *Of Albert* have been poor, Andrew Ridgeley still finds himself benefiting financially to the tune of £10,000 per annum from his share of 'Careless Whisper''s royalties alone.

VIDEOS

Look out for the following themes that are prevalent in the majority of the videos: bottoms, tartan, bad hair days and walls used for emotional support.

Wham! The Video
(SONY VHS 498482 / CBS/FOX VHS 3048-50)

Wham! Rap / Club Tropicana / Wake Me Up Before You Go-Go / Careless Whisper / Last Christmas

Wham! Rap

The promo clip accompanying Wham!'s re-released début single shows George and Andrew as rebellious teenagers, defying their parents' wishes and enjoying life on the dole. George's ponytailed strut and the depiction of 'Mr Average' are as hilariously dated as the boys' stonewashed, three quarter length jeans. Shirlie and D C Lee make an early appearance pair-dancing with the boys, and the gross caricature of the parents combine to make a lively, gently alternative video. Note that George cheekily shows off his leather-clad bottom for the first time!

Club Tropicana

The lyrical parody of 'Club Tropicana' was intended to be exaggerated by the video, which was luxuriously shot in the sun-drenched Balearic Islands. Expanses of well-oiled flesh are on display around the poolside and George and Andrew frolic in the apparent lap of luxury, sporting deep suntans and sparkling white teeth. After various encounters between the Wham! boys and the backing girls, the foursome dress up in airline uniforms, thus dispelling any implications that they are actually rich jet setters. George jumps at the opportunity to fulfil a childhood ambition by becoming a pilot for the day.

Wake Me Up Before You Go-Go

Having decided to go for a more accessible dance video, Wham! invited hundreds of fans to be extras in this athletic promo with the sole proviso that they came dressed in white, wearing fluorescent accessories. The colourful effect perfectly accompanies the song's infectious appeal, with a dramatic change to ultraviolet light towards the climax of the song. Pop's prime moment occurs when George hugs himself with his Day-Glo yellow fingerless gloves and rolls his eyes skywards in a smarmy attempt at seduction: 'It's cold out there / But it's warm in bed / They can dance / We'll stay home instead'.

Careless Whisper

George's first solo video hit the headlines for its saucy adultery, with the much publicised rumour that model Lisa Stahl had fainted during a particularly passionate scene with George. A second film was then shot as the first was deemed too racy, and as George declared, 'I'm always very careful what my fans see. I did think the video needed some changes'... all we see now is a tame kiss on the neck. Equally newsworthy was the extortionate expense as the video shoot went £17,000 over budget when George called in his hairdresser sister Melanie to calm his frizzy mane, which had been aggravated by Miami's intense humidity.

Last Christmas

'Last Christmas' sees Wham! and a group of friends arriving at a picturesque log cabin for their annual Yuletide get-together. George is tormented by seeing his ex-girlfriend with Andrew, and she becomes the subject of many rueful glances. The festive merriment continues around him regardless and Andrew makes his first appearance in tartan, albeit of a snowy variety.

Wham! '85

(SONY VHS 498462 / CBS/FOX VHS 3075-50)

Everything She Wants / Freedom / I'm Your Man

Everything She Wants

This black and white film based on concert footage, with heavily overdubbed crowd noise visually reflects the improved quality of Wham!'s work. Personally edited by George, the video opens with a spectacular curtain drop to reveal George's new, mature Bee Gee-ish look and Andrew's growing obsession with tartan. George fixes the camera with a piercing stare and delivers his tale of marital strife with sincerity, whilst Andrew busies himself with astounding triple high jumps. If you thought the energetic gymnastics on 'Go-Go' were exciting, then you ain't seen nothing yet!

Freedom

After the initial video was abandoned, Wham! decided to use clips from the China tour to promote their single, 'Freedom'. The film begins with George and Andrew debating the triumphs and failings of the trip against the background music of Richard Hartley. Although most of the footage is available on the *Foreign Skies* video, it somehow becomes more meaningful when summed up within a four-minute pop video. The ever fashion conscious Andrew models no less than five different tartan designs.

I'm Your Man

Filmed at London's Marquee Club in Wardour Street, 'I'm Your Man' opens with George and Andrew in an excruciatingly stilted sketch, desperately trying to tout the remaining tickets for the concert that night. The band puts on a cocky display of macho camaraderie with endless mugging-up to the camera. A mock film countdown is superimposed over the screen, sending subtle sex messages to the viewer.

Wham! In China –
Foreign Skies

(TECHNICOLOR VHS 714250 / CBS/FOX VHS
7142.50)

Tony Parsons accurately comments in *Bare*, 'Like the trip itself, *Foreign Skies* is a sad, confused affair.' Wham!'s ground-breaking but ill-fated invasion of China paradoxically cost the group and their management a cool £1 million. The whole event was filmed as a documentary by director Lindsay Anderson, whose previous credentials included *If...* and *O! Lucky Man,* but following artistic differences Anderson and Wham! parted company. This left the boys, Jazz Summers and Martin Lewis to complete the editing, although the credits describe the picture as a 'Lindsay Anderson Film'.

Wham!'s fleeting impact on China was phenomenal as they amply lived up to the direct translation of their name, 'Wei Meng', meaning 'powerful and vigorous'!

Not all conversions were accurate though and 'Go-Go' was endearingly reviewed as 'Wake Me Up Before You Leave' by the China News Service. The oppression of the Chinese authorities is painfully apparent in the film, portrayed in one instance by a grim-faced official switching off a harmless Wham! video that had been enjoyed by a group of men. While 'Love Machine' was banned for being too raunchy, the audience was warned not to dance or clap and plenty of security guards are seen to be present in *Foreign Skies* to enforce this rule.

Nomis invited four British tabloid journalists with them at the cost of £10,000 each, who are depicted in the film as news-hungry menials. George was visibly irritated by the ever-present camera while Andrew lapped up the constant attention, coming across as charming but vain. Highlights include the body popper Trevor Duncan, the boys playing football and the cringe-making superficiality of the British Ambassador's drinks party – bring out the Ferrero Rocher! The majority of the music performed was from the first two albums, supported by the energetic Pepsi and Shirlie except for George's slower solo performance, where he is tantalisingly dressed in a white suit minus the shirt.

Originally grandly titled 'Wham! In China! A Cultural Revolution', the documentary was later blandly renamed *Foreign Skies*, and was first shown at *The Final* concert, later followed by an inconsequential video release. Despite its flaws, the film is a candid insight into the tour as Andrew Ridgeley rightly sums up; 'I don't think it matters that we look all ragged and pale and un-pop star like. It remains a unique event.'

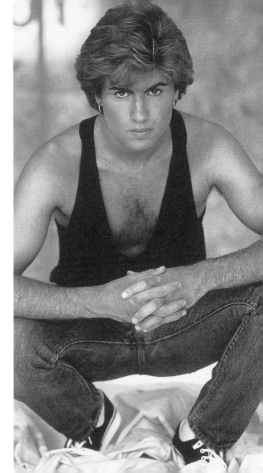

Wham! The Final

(SONY VHS 498472 / CBS/FOX VHS 3846.50)

The Edge Of Heaven / A Different Corner / Where Did Your Heart Go?

The Edge Of Heaven

Directed by George and Andy Morahan, Wham!'s action packed video for 'The Edge Of Heaven' is an elegant cross between a Marquee styled rock performance and sentimental footage of Wham!'s career. The audience comprised 300 students from the Epsom College of Art who earned £30 for their enthusiastic cheering and dancing. The band's high sprits make for a climactic final promo despite the poignant ghost of a clock ticking away and the touching farewell 'GOODBYE' scrolling across the screen.

A Different Corner

Possibly his worst video, 'A Different Corner' shows a long-haired George in a sterile white environment which is unfortunately reminiscent of a padded cell. As if his patterned white cardigan (read straight jacket) wasn't bad enough, George clings to a pole, leans against a wall and rocks himself obsessively. The excitement ends there.

Where Did Your Heart Go?

Tassels akimbo, the band are half hidden in moody shadows while George flamboyantly strikes a single snare drum. 'Where Did Your Heart Go?' is worth watching just for Andrew's staggeringly impassioned miming and George's stunning shoulder shuffles in dramatic silhouette.

Faith
(SONY VHS 49000 2)

I Want Your Sex (Uncensored Version) / Faith / Father Figure / One More Try / Monkey / Kissing A Fool

Faith showcases six promotional videos from the album and also includes interview footage of George. He speaks animatedly about each of the songs in between clips, which conspicuously contrasts his pronounced English accent with the hugely Americanised promos. The picture is also very distracting as it constantly swaps from side to side and changes colour, presumably in an attempt to spice up the nondescript interview setting.

I Want Your Sex (Uncensored Version)

'I Want Your Sex' shows George and long-time girlfriend Kathy Jeung in intimate relations, with her dressing up in lingerie, high heels and a wig to please her partner. 'Careless Whisper' was never as risqué as this, with the couple's erotic imagery involving blindfolds, water and silken sheets. George is careful to reinforce the safe sex message, as he writes the words 'Explore Monogamy' in lipstick on Kathy's thigh and back. However openly sexual George was prepared to be, he didn't go as far as appearing naked in the film, thanks to stand-in Chris Beedie. George joked in *Bare*, 'Anyone who thought that strapping lad baring all in 'Sex' was me was sadly mistaken. Ever met a Greek without a hairy chest? And anyway, if I'd been doing it, I wouldn't have been able to watch it, would I?'

Faith

Beginning with the remnants of 'I Want Your Sex' as played on a jukebox, 'Faith' is a totally different affair with George making the transition from lover to rock 'n' roll star. He dons an array of Fifties attire including steel capped cowboy boots, shades, faded torn jeans, and a leather jacket symbolically adorned with a string of pearls to show his more feminine side. For fans of George's highly acclaimed bottom, this is a treat!

Father Figure

'Father Figure' is a veritable epic. Starring Vogue model Tania Coleridge, the saga follows George, the New York cabbie whose fantasy is bedding the budding starlet he chauffeurs. Not only does he want to be her lover, George also wishes to protect her, but throughout the course of the video she grows up and rejects all her potential father figures. *Top Of The Pops* vetoed the steamy and passionate bedroom scenes, instead using an obscure one minute excerpt to promote the single. Rumours abounded that George had ditched Kathy for Tania, proposing an exotic holiday which Tania's real life father (figure) vehemently denied in the tabloids.

One More Try

It seems that George cannot stand on his own two feet, relying on the presence of a wall to aid him in this otherwise life-less, static clip. The only glimmer of action is when he draws a broken heart on the steamed-up mirror. One to miss.

Monkey

This is the Jimmy Jam and Terry Lewis mix that topped the US charts and is therefore different to the track that appears on the album. 'Monkey' is based on a powerfully energetic live performance, interspersed by equally vibrant scenes of George strutting his stuff, fetchingly decked out in Eighties braces and hat. He dances provoca-tively with backing singer Lynn Mabry and then gamely sprints across the stage to lark around with ever-present Deon Estus.

Kissing A Fool

This is set in a smoky jazz club, accu-rately capturing the feel of the song. A standard but effective promo that for some reason was omitted from the US release of this video.

George Michael
(SONY VHS 49063 2)

George Michael was chosen as the first artist to be interviewed for a new series of the gritty television institution known as *The South Bank Show* with Melvyn Bragg, in order to increase the programme's flagging ratings. Bragg introduces his subject as the 'most successful pop artist of the decade' and there follows an uncharacteristically gushy interview skimming over thorny issues and concentrating purely on George's creative abilities (strictly in accordance with the star's wishes). The interview took place in and around the studio during the recording of his public coming-of-age album, *Listen Without Prejudice Volume I*, and was simultaneously released as the televisual equivalent, alongside his autobiography with Tony Parsons, *Bare*.

George appears relaxed and at ease, dressed in trendy sports clothes and enthusiastic about all aspects of his songwriting and influences. Among the interviewees only Simon Napier-Bell takes a negative stance, while a clip of Gladys Knight is shown criticising George for his universal appeal in winning a traditionally black R&B award. The ghost of Andrew Ridgeley is finally exorcised as his presence is saliently absent throughout this promotional piece. *George Michael* was duly packaged and marketed as a Christmas stocking filler thus trivialising the once scathing essence of *The South Bank Show*.

Wham! – Best Of
(SONY VHS 2007772)

Wham! Rap / Club Tropicana / Wake Me Up Before You Go-Go / Last Christmas / The Edge Of Heaven / Where Did Your Heart Go? / I'm Your Man / Everything She Wants / Freedom

Released in tandem with *The Best of Wham! – If You Were There*, this video sadly ensured the deletion of previous Wham! promo packages. Although featuring the same cover design as the CD, there are fewer tracks making a slightly short 'Best Of' compilation. Enjoyable nonetheless.

INDEX